Harley-Davidson

Doug Mitchel

First published in 2007 by Motorbooks, an imprint
of MBI Publishing Company, 400 First Avenue
North, Suite 300, Minneapolis, MN 55401 USA.

The information in this book is true and complete
to the best of our knowledge. All
recommendations are made without any guarantee
on the part of the author or Publisher, who also
disclaim any liability incurred in connection with
the use of this data or specific details.

This publication has been prepared solely by MBI
Publishing Company and is not approved or
licensed by any other entity. We recognize that
some words, model names, and designations
mentioned herein are the property of the
trademark holder. We use them for identification
purposes only. This is not an official publication.

Motorbooks titles are also available at discounts in
bulk quantity for industrial or sales-promotional
use. For details write to Special Sales Manager at
MBI Publishing Company, 400 First Avenue
North, Suite 300, Minneapolis, MN 55401 USA.

To find out more about our books, join us online
at www.motorbooks.com.

Editor: Peter Schletty
Designer: Maria Friedrich

Mitchel, Doug.
  Harley-Davidson / by Doug Mitchel.
    p. cm.
  Includes index.
  ISBN-13: 978-0-7603-2991-7 (softbound)
  ISBN-10: 0-7603-2991-5 (softbound)
  1. Harley Davidson motorcycle--History. 2.
Harley Davidson
motorcycle--Pictorial works. I. Title.
  TL448.H3 M5695
  629.227'5--dc22   2007006296

About the Author
Doug Mitchel is a writer and photographer
specializing in Harley-Davidson motorcycles. He
lives in Aurora, Illinois.

On the front cover: The 2007 Road King Classic
touring motorcycle. *Photo by Kevin Wing*

On the frontispiece: Introduced in 1999, the
Twin-Cam 88 motor delivered a new level of power
and smoothness.

On the title page: Heavily accessorized, this 1941
EL is a prime example of what an owner could add
to his Harley in the day.

On the back cover, left: Continued use of colorful
tank graphics adds to the allure of the latest models
in the Harley catalog. **Middle:** Still carbureted in
1994, the Evo motor was nonetheless a potent
powerplant. **Right:** The number 1 on the fuel tank
of this 35th Anniversary Super Glide is a strong
reminder of the past.

Printed in China

Contents

Introduction

The turn of the last century would prove to be a tumultuous period for the eager inventors who rushed to build their own version of the two-wheeled contraptions we call motorcycles. With a limited availability of off-the-shelf components, those without a high degree of both engineering and marketing savvy found themselves out of business as quickly as they began. The United States had nearly 300 makers of these spindly, underpowered machines, but only a handful survived their first days of creation.

Of these attempts, one was crafted by a pair of boyhood chums who were also neighbors and coworkers. Young and energetic, William S. Harley and Arthur Davidson witnessed the birth of motorcycling in 1901 and were eager to join their talents to create one of their own. Harley had an extensive background in engineering, while Davidson was more of a hands-on guy who could create the required tooling. Working in a small wooden shed behind the Davidson home, the boys were soon joined by two more Davidsons as the project progressed. This innocent band of men would go on to create not just another brand of motorcycle, but an American icon. It's doubtful that even in their youthful exuberance they could have foretold what would become a legendary brand in the field of motorcycling.

Their first effort was similar to many others being built, since technology and hardware options were few. About all they had to offer was a single-cylinder motor bolted to a fortified bicycle frame. The basic black paint was adorned with the now classic Harley-Davidson name on only one side of the angular fuel tank, but it was all that was required to roll the company into the history books. That machine has come to be known as Serial Number One, and the fully restored machine is now on display for the world to see at the corporate headquarters in Milwaukee, Wisconsin.

With wide-eyed innocence and a desire to succeed, Harley and Davidson set into action their plans to sell a motorcycle bearing their names. Although a total of three Davidsons and only one Harley were involved, the order of family names was chosen due to the high degree of engineering brought to the table by William Harley. With William's engineering background playing the major role in the design, it was only fitting that his name be first in the company moniker. This was in spite of the fact that three members of the Davidson family joined the fray at the earliest stage, thus proving the value of a sound design and its creator.

Early efforts of the boys were marred by failure, yet they refused to give in to such minor setbacks. Turning to a friend and mentor named Ole Evinrude for guidance, the team learned of improved methods for building a motor. Air cooling was chosen over the previous liquid-cooled route to save weight and complexity. The results of their improved design yielded a displacement of 24.74 inches and a horsepower rating of 3. Hardly the power that dreams are made of, but dependability was a required parameter from the start.

Having addressed and amended the initial engine needs, their next conflict came with the frame that would carry the new motor. Early efforts in engine design allowed a standard bicycle frame to carry the load, but their enhanced mill was too much for any existing bike chassis.

Other builders were experimenting with improved designs of their own, and the Harley-Davidson crew followed in their footsteps to create a unit that was capable of holding the single-cylinder powerplant firmly in its grasp. With motor and chassis dilemmas now firmly in hand, little was left to complete the assembly of their first "production" motorcycle. The entire process took months to complete, but they were soon seen tooling around the rough streets of Milwaukee aboard their new creation.

The years that followed saw numerous, yet incremental, improvements to their first motorcycle. The sparse record keeping of the period preserved few details of their engineering progress, and the passing of time has all but eliminated these. Remaining examples of the earliest machines, however, provide evidence enough of their ongoing enhancements.

With William Harley returning to school to expand his knowledge, and still no record of changes, it is hard to say how many 1904 models were assembled. Today's estimates put the number somewhere in the single digit range. But even then, changes to the 1903 were more than likely minimal at best.

As availability of new materials and technology grew, so did the efforts of the original crew and their two-wheeled creation. It would take several years, but a V-twin motor was finally created that delivered the power and reliability that was demanded from the makers and their buyers. Once the engine layout was created, there was no looking back, and Harley-Davidsons have become known for their thumping V-twin mills. A few attempts were made to install an alternate motor into the frames, but those never caught on and were quickly scrapped.

Even having accepted the V-twin configuration as its own, Harley-Davidson continued to improve the breed with every new iteration of the motor. Some changes were more dramatic than others, but every step taken made the machines more powerful and more reliable. With newer and better motors, the style and contours of the overall machines grew into the classic lines we know today.

Chapter One: The Early Days

Surviving and even prospering during the passing of two world wars, the Motor Company found itself under siege from another foe: imported motorcycles. The arrival of Honda in 1959, and others soon after, put Harley-Davidson under a pressure it had never before experienced. Seeking respite from this new scourge, Harley joined ranks with a corporate giant named AMF. While the deep pockets of its new partner made life a bit more livable, the higher production numbers were achieved at the cost of quality, and the Motor Company began to lose its long-standing reputation as a builder of dependable motorcycles. H-D would go on to survive the team effort and regain its independence in time to salvage the name. Government assistance came in the form of tariffs against the larger Asian machines some time later, but this situation was short-lived, as Harley was coming into its own by the end of the 1980s.

By the time its 90th birthday rolled into view, Harley-Davidson was experiencing a robust period of growth that not even the founders could have foreseen. The public celebration held in Milwaukee to mark the anniversary was attended by hundreds of thousands of fans, proving to the world that perhaps the firm had at last arrived. Over 100 years the name Harley-Davidson became one of the most recognized brands in the world. Buying demand has often resulted in lengthy waiting lists at local dealers as customers satisfy their need for a Milwaukee-built cycle.

The Motor Company has traveled some rocky roads in its day, but it's been transformed into a modern example of how a motorcycle company should be run. The advent of technology plays into the production of each of the latest machines, but the basic form remains true to the early creations people have come to know and love. New models roll off the assembly lines every year as the Motor Company grows its appeal to a wider audience. Although production seems to have caught up with the needs of buyers, the company and its stock continue to march upward with no sign of abatement in sight. Considering its humble beginnings, that is a feat that is not easily repeated, and seldom successful.

The 1910 Model 6 included a belt idler control, allowing the rider to remove tension from the drive belt while the motor continued to run.

Still wearing the original paint, this 1905 Model 1 gives us a glimpse at the past before the restoration process changes it into a gleaming museum piece.

Year: 1905
Model: Model 1
Engine: Single-cylinder, 26.84 cubic inches
Transmission: None
Features: Three-coil saddle

The leather drive belt was the only means of delivering energy from the motor to the rear wheel.

Powered by a single-cylinder motor that produced about 3 horsepower, the 1905 Model 1 was typical of motorcycles of the day.

The first print ads for Harley-Davidson Motor Cycle Motors were seen in 1905 and would open the first doors to the corridors of history. A slightly larger bore in the single-cylinder motor resulted in an increase in power to 3 1/4 horsepower from the 26.84-inch displacement. The fuel tank was still fastened to the tubular frame with polished straps of steel, later earning them their "strap tank" nickname.

The success of the brand was growing rapidly, even in the infancy of the company. The single-cylinder motor would soldier on for several more years, but gain in dependability with every passing model year. With outside interest in the offerings expanding, 1905 was considered to be the first true year of production, but it would certainly not be the last.

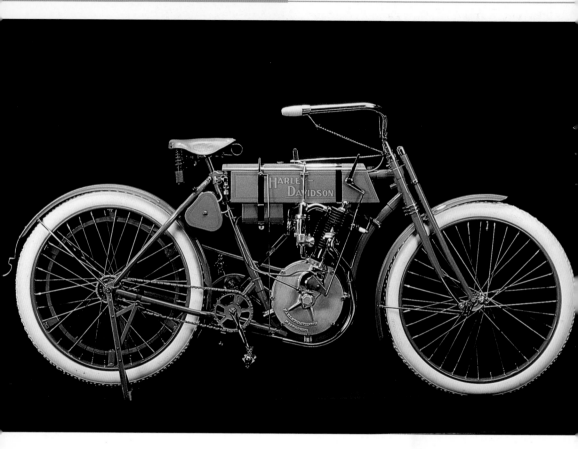

Changes from year-to-year in the early stages of the Motor Company models were few, but the 1907 crankcase was assembled with eight bolts versus the six of 1906.

Year: 1907
Model: Model 3
Engine: Single-cylinder, 26.84 cubic inches
Transmission: None
Features: Sprung forks

The Model 2 was introduced in 1906, with only minor alterations. Larger changes were being made to the workshop and assembly process, as space was quickly becoming an issue.

Expansion continued in 1907, including the first incorporation and stock offering. Additional funding was raised to provide for a larger two-story building and a tripling of staff. These efforts would allow for 150 Model 3 units to be assembled that year.

Only minor revisions were made to the 1907 Model 3, but bigger changes were soon to be implemented. As they produced more machines, greater space and capital needs were addressed as the fledgling firm began to take shape. Once in motion, progress would come quickly, as motorcycles grew in popularity and were pressed into service by a wide variety of buyers.

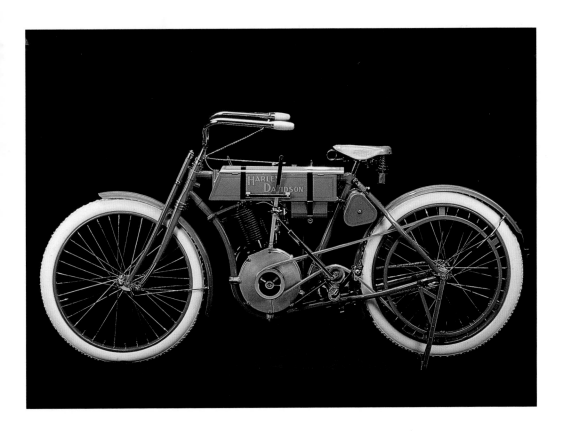

Still belt driven in 1907, the machine was just as prone to slippage when wet as it had been in the first year of production.

Model 6C had a set of 26-inch wheels and a magneto ignition, one of four variations sold in that year.

Year: 1910
Model: Model 6C
Engine: Single-cylinder, 30.16 cubic inches
Transmission: None
Features: 26-inch wheels and magneto ignition

Revisions to the tank mounting saw the removal of the previous steel straps, while the flat-sided design remained.

Improvements for 1910 included the addition of a belt idler control, allowing the rider to remove tension from the drive belt while the motor continued to run. This feature was considered a great boon to the rider's comfort and ease of operation, making two-wheeled transportation more appealing than ever.

Fuel tanks, now installed without the steel straps, retained the angular contours of the earlier models. Options carried over from the 1909 models included battery or magneto ignitions and a choice of 26- or 28-inch wheels.

Despite only minor changes to the lineup, Harley-Davidson offered four model variations and sold more than 3,000 copies in a single year. Prices remained the same for the 1910s, adding value to the buyer's equation.

New for 1910 was the belt idler lever that permitted the rider to eliminate tension from the drive belt while the motor continued to run.

This 1911 Model 7A wears the larger 28-inch wheels and is fitted with a magneto ignition.

At long last, Harley-Davidson added a V-twin to its lineup in 1911. Previous encounters with a two-cylinder motor had proved unworthy of the name, but the bugs had been worked out and the Model 7D carried 50 inches of displacement in the 45-degree motor. The production V-twin carried a price tag of $300 on a pair of 28-inch wheels.

Four single-cylinder models remained on the roster, again with battery or magneto, and 26- or 28-inch rims. Additional cooling fins were added to the cylinders to improve temperature control, as the subtle tweaks continued to boost the image of the brand.

While Harley-Davidson was busy expanding production and improving the breed, private owners were racing and winning astride the Milwaukee-built machines. The factory had no intentions of starting a racing effort, but encouraged and appreciated those who won aboard their cycles.

The inclusion of additional fins on the motor's casting delivered improved cooling as the machines were being put into heavier use.

Year: 1911
Model: 7A
Engine: Single-cylinder, 30.16 cubic inches
Transmission: None, belt-drive idler
Features: 28-inch wheels and magneto ignition

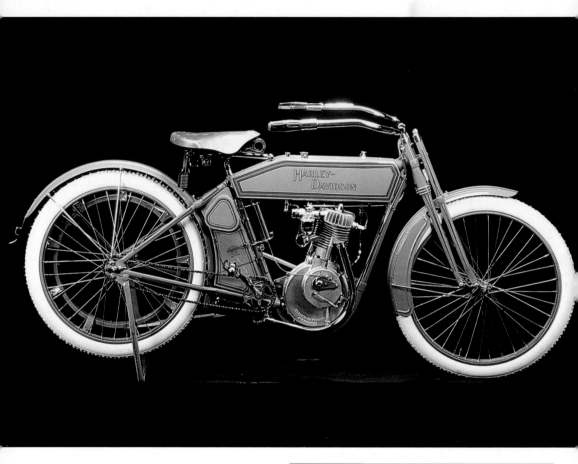

The 1912 models wore altered frame tubes that delivered a lower seat height along with a few additional minor upgrades.

Year: **1912**
Model: **8**
Engine: **Single-cylinder, 30.16 cubic inches**
Transmission: **None, belt-drive idler**
Features: **Battery ignition**

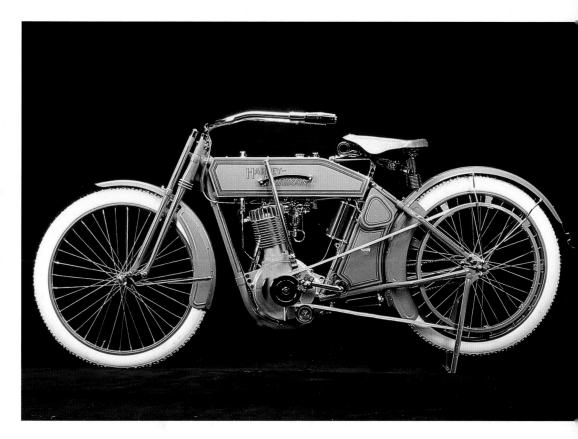

Hoping to aid riders in the comfort department with its 1912 models, Harley featured an upper frame tube that provided a lower saddle height. Further measures were taken by adding a spring to the vertical frame tube, thus delivering some movement to the saddle.

A simple clutch could be added to the rear wheel to allow for smoother takeoff from a stopped position, another first for the maker. Pedals were still employed, but were now much easier to adjust, delivering more ease to the latest crop of buyers.

Four single-cylinder and a trio of twin-cylinder models filled the catalog pages, offering more choices than ever for the growing motorcycle audience. Prices continued to climb, but any model in the 1912 lineup could be ridden home for less than $300.

In addition to the lower seat height, a spring mounted in the vertical frame tube permitted a few inches of travel and a higher degree of comfort for the rider.

The Harley-Davidson catalog grew with every model year, and the 1914 10C was one of six variations being sold.

Until the 1913 models arrived, all Harley-Davidsons had been fitted with a final drive belt fashioned of leather. The new Model 9s sported an optional chain drive that eliminated the slippage of the wide leather belts for more confident delivery of the slowly increasing horsepower. Continued improvements on the 1914 Model 10 included a step-starter and a two-speed rear hub.

The two-speed transmission brought new sophistication to the 10C as well as added flexibility to the ride and its uses. Steel floorboards also added convenience to the overall quality of the experience.

The foot-operated brake pedal was another new item which helped the pilot slow the 1914 model down from speed. The 35-cubic-inch motor delivered more power when accelerating. Overall, the Harley-Davidson line was improving with every passing year, adding new buyers to the fold.

With chain drive finally being offered as an option in 1913, more and more buyers were choosing the new system.

Year: 1914
Model: 10C
Engine: Single-cylinder, 35 cubic inches
Transmission: Two-speed, in rear hub
Features: Chain drive

Since the motorcycle's first appearance, people have been racing them as privateers. Harley-Davidson offered a factory race machine in the form of this 1914 board track model.

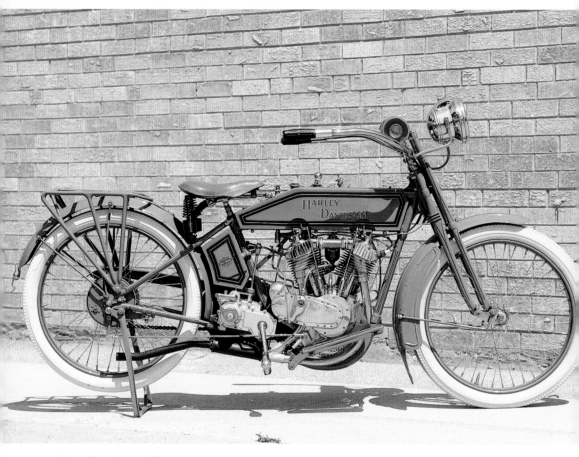

Harley offered 16 different models in 1915, and the 11F carried the all new, three-speed gearbox in its frame rails.

Nineteen fifteen would see the installation of a true three-speed gearbox, along with a guaranteed 11 horsepower from the twin-cylinder motor of the 1915 Model 11. The 11E was equipped with a two-speed gearbox and the 11F seen here carries a third gear in the newly mounted case resting behind the motor.

Although electric lighting was being offered on some models, this 11F still carries the acetylene-powered arrangement. The cylindrical tank on the handlebars holds the required fuel and distributes it to the lights on demand.

Selling for $275, the 11F was ridden out the door by nearly 10,000 buyers for the model year, making it the most popular Harley in the line.

Having the choice between single- and twin-cylinder motors, most Harley buyers leaned toward the latter, and just over 60 inches of displacement was their reward.

Year: 1915
Model: 11F
Engine: Twin-cylinder, 60.34 cubic inches
Transmission: three-speed
Features: Acetylene lighting

Selling nearly 10,000 11Fs for the model year made the three-speed version Harley's best seller.

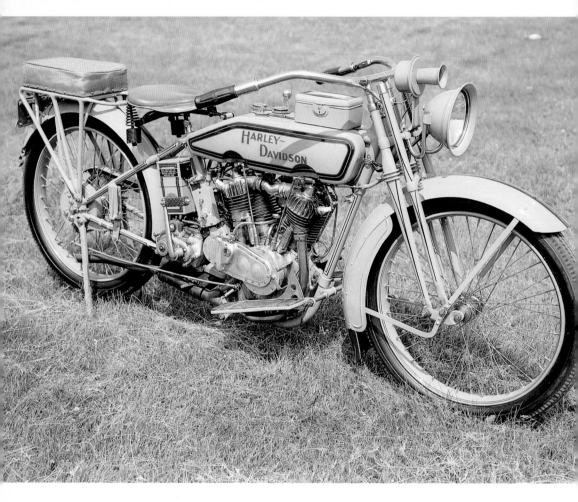

The 1916 J model was Harley's second-best seller for that year, with nearly 6,000 copies produced.

Year: **1916**
Model: **16J**
Engine: **Twin-cylinder, 60.34 cubic inches**
Transmission: **Three-speed**
Features: **Electric system**

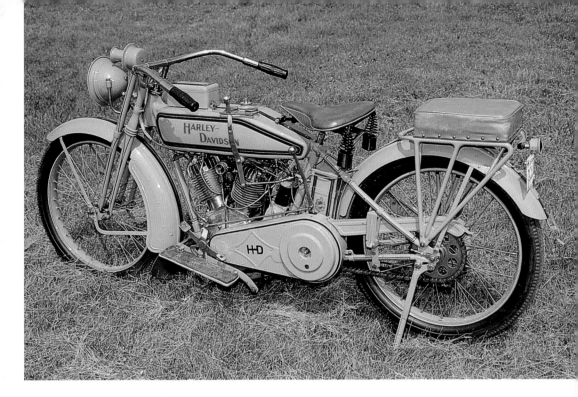

The 1916 models were different in several ways, and showed further improvement over their predecessors. For the first time in Harley production, the same frame was used for either the single- or twin-cylinder models. This allowed for a more streamlined assembly line and reduced inventory.

Fuel and oil tanks were also modified and were far more sculpted than the previous editions. Additional capacity was also gained by the new shapes, thus allowing the rider and a passenger to travel over longer distances between fuel stops.

Nineteen sixteen also marked the first year when model numbers coincided with the model year. This would help to clarify future listings in the sales catalogs and make it far easier for people to keep the annual changes in order.

Decked out with a three-speed gearbox, electric lights, and a deeply padded passenger pillion, this 16J is ready for anything.

The 60.34-cubic-inch F-head motor was mounted beneath a new fuel tank design that was sleeker and could carry more fuel.

Sales of the 1917 Model F came in second only to the Model J of the same year, and lacked only the J's electrics.

As the popularity of Harley-Davidson grew, so did uses for the nimble two-wheeled machines. From this growth came the need for better machines, and the 1917 models gained internal modifications that bolstered their abilities.

The twin-cylinder models benefited from a four-lobe cam setup that had previously only been seen on the eight-valve race bikes.

With World War I looming large on the horizon, a new green color was applied to Harley-Davidsons as a show of support for the U.S. troops. The 17F sat just below the 17J in sales, and the only difference was the electric lights on the J version. More than 8,500 copies of the 17F were produced that model year, carrying an MSRP of $275.

Year: 1917
Model: 17F
Engine: Twin-cylinder, 60.34 cubic inches
Transmission: Three-speed
Features: Green paint

Simplicity and durability were both mainstays of the entire Harley-Davidson lineup, and the Model F embodied that spirit.

This Model C is powered by a single-cylinder motor and carries a passenger in the stylish wicker sidecar.

In 1919, Harley-Davidson introduced its WF model, powered by a horizontally opposed twin-cylinder motor.

Year: 1919
Model: WF or Sport
Engine: Horizontally opposed
   twin-cylinder, 35.64 cubic inches
Transmission: Three-speed
Features: Streamlined fuel tank

The approach of World War I would hamper extensive R&D efforts, but units continued to roll off the assembly line. The war took its toll on civilian production, and in 1918 the government pressed 20,000 Harley-Davidsons into duty. These limiting factors did not keep the engineering team at Harley from crafting new machines. The Sport models, introduced in 1919, featured horizontally-opposed motors for the first time in a Harley frame. The radical new design was not warmly received by members of the riding public, who had already earned a deep-seated affection for the 45-degree V-twin motor.

The opposed motor displaced 35.64 cubic inches in total and shifted through a three-speed gearbox. Fewer than 800 units were built for the first year, even though it was the least expensive model in the truncated catalog of the World War I era.

Displacing a total of 35.64 inches, the pair of opposed cylinders ran inline with the chassis, but proved to be less than popular among Harley buyers.

The WF or Sport models were a radical departure in Harley design, and illustrated the company's willingness to try new technology.

Chapter Two: The '20s Roar In

The period from 1903 to the 1920s was one of fast-paced changes for both Harley-Davidson and the rest of the fledgling motorcycle industry. The fact that this two-wheeled craft had even grown into an industry surprised many who viewed the vehicles as pure folly.

The early part of the 1900s would prove to be a fertile arena for new blood as every guy with a dream and a wrench rushed to build his own version of a motorcycle. For whatever reason, 98 percent of these early efforts died on the vine while Harley-Davidson grew beyond its expectations and was soon viewed as the leader of the pack.

Beginning the trek with a single-cylinder motor was typical for the day, but Harley soon toyed with the option of putting a twin-cylinder mill into the frames of its machines. Early efforts were stymied by the lack of technology, but stubborn persistence rewarded the crew with a working design in 1909. While a great leap forward, the motor did not fill all of Harley's demands, and would disappear until its return in 1911. Once the format was proven to be viable,

yearly alterations made the new motor a better breed. People loved the power they got from having a pair of cylinders, and the demand for the single-cylinder models began to wane.

Having chosen the 45-degree layout early on, most of the two-cylinder motors retained that configuration. Additional upgrades continued to enhance the performance and reliability of the motor, but Harley also toyed with alternatives to the now classic V-twin. The Sport model, introduced in 1919, carried a horizontally opposed powerplant in the frame. The motor was glassy smooth, but buyers shunned the radical nature of the beast and stuck to their V-twin buying plans.

Of course, a motorcycle is more than its motor, and Harley pressed on to improve every facet of their bikes' designs. A two-speed hub was seen in 1914, and the leather belt drives were supplanted by chains at the same time. Although the new drive system was a bit messier, it was far more reliable, especially when riding in the wet. Suspension improvements made their way into the mix, bringing new levels of comfort to both the rider and passenger. As the motorcycle was earning respect as a useful device, Harley-Davidson made great strides to make it as user-friendly as possible. Optional electric lighting and with a three-speed gearbox in 1915 were proof that Harley was not content to rest on the laurels of previous successes.

Adding to the changes that were visible to the naked eye, enhancements were also being employed in the internal workings of the motor and gearbox. New metal hardening processes delivered exceptional longevity to their already time-tested designs. These improvements drew more people to the showrooms as they grew more confident in the viability of the two-wheeled format as a day-to-day method of transportation.

While Harley-Davidson was making every effort to build a dependable machine, the competition dwindled. By the time 1920 arrived, the throng of American motorcycle builders had shrunk from several hundred to only a handful, with Harley-Davidson in the lead.

The 1924 Harley-Davidson sales catalog featured 14 different models, including the JE, which featured aluminum pistons.

The 60.34-cubic-inch motor of the J now featured revised contours on the cooling fins that surrounded the spark plugs.

Only tiny changes were made to the 1920 models, although their presence made for an improved machine.

Harley-Davidson's continued efforts during World War I placed the company in a strong position when the conflict ended in 1918. By 1920, as Harley and the other remaining U.S. builders again turned to the civilian market, the Milwaukee firm found itself in the lead.

The 1920 models from Harley carried a raft of small changes, most of which were inside the motor's cases. New cylinder castings were introduced to make the motor run smoother. The new castings would still require some of the cylinders to carry compression plates to equal out the reading inside each jug.

Plant capacity also grew to 542,000 square feet, making it the largest motorcycle manufacturing facility in the country. Even Harley's rival, Indian Motocycles, was using a factory that measured 520,000 square feet, giving an indication of things to come.

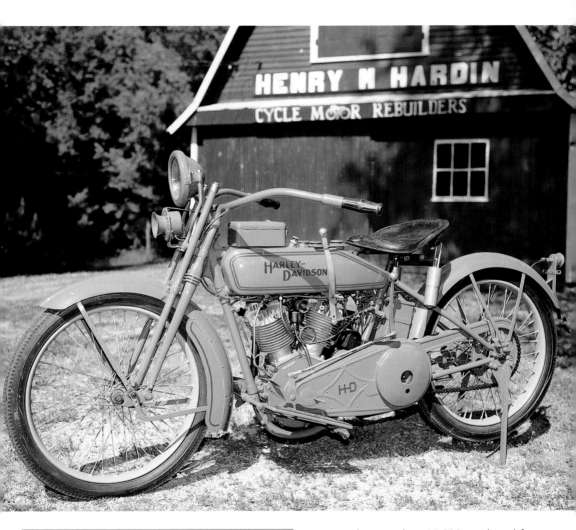

Year: 1920
Model: 20J
Engine: Twin-cylinder, 60.34 cubic inches
Transmission: Three-speed
Features: Electric lighting

With more than 14,000 produced for 1920, the J was far and away Harley's most popular model.

Year: 1922
Model: JD
Engine: Twin-cylinder, 61 cubic inches
Transmission: Single-speed
Features: Capable of exceeding 100
    miles per hour, no brakes

In the heyday of board track racing, the JD had done its share of damage with Harley's "Wrecking Crew" aboard the powerful machines.

The 61-cubic-inch motor of the race-bred JD exhaled through a truncated set of exhaust pipes that often belched flames during the race and while being warmed up in the pits prior to the event.

Lacking brakes and a throttle, the 1922 JD was either "on" or "off" and could reach speeds of 100 miles per hour on a wooden track.

Built to continue the reign of domination that the factory race team had already earned, the 1922 Model JD was sent to board tracks around the country. The powerful 61-cubic-inch

motor put the JD into the crowd pleasing 1,000-cc class, and it often rolled home carrying another trophy.

Board track racing was highly dangerous, made partly so because the machines that participated carried no form of braking and very little, if any, suspension. The protective clothing of the day was limited to long-sleeve shirts, leather helmets, and a set of goggles. While traveling at speeds that often exceeded 100 miles per hour, any mishap during the race would prove to be painful, if not fatal.

As successful as the Harley-Davidson "Wrecking Crew" had become, this form of racing was soon to be deemed too dangerous for the racers and the crowds, as several spectators had been killed or seriously injured during a racing mishap.

The F-head twin motor remained a popular choice among buyers, especially in the 74-inch variety.

Due to the revised frame, bodywork, and overall styling, the 1925 models cast an entirely new shadow on the market.

In an effort to staunch the loss of buyers to the four-wheeled showrooms, Harley introduced a new and improved line of models in 1925. The frames were now lower, making them accessible to more riders and "new low prices" were posted in hopes of drawing more buyers to the fold. Sleeker sheet metal also gave them a sportier look, while a raft of minor mechanical upgrades helped make them better machines with easier maintenance. The 25JD was the top-selling model for 1925, with more than 9,500 units leaving the factory.

It carried in its frame the larger 74-cubic-inch motor and the three-speed gearbox. Electric lighting allowed it to be ridden after dark. The tubular steel toolbox and vertical battery storage compartment were two more of the revised styling cues of the 1925 models.

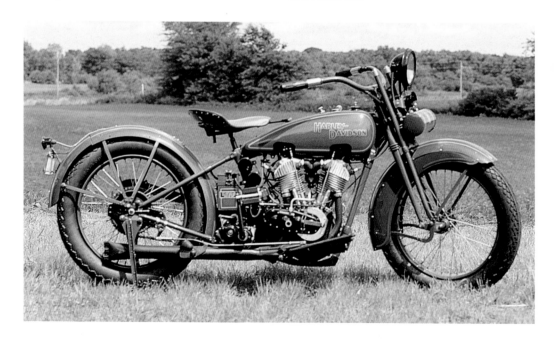

Introduced with revised frames and sheet metal, the 1925 models looked and rode better than their predecessors.

Year: 1925
Model: 25JD
Engine: Twin-cylinder, 74 cubic inches
Transmission: Three-speed
Features: All new sheet metal and frame

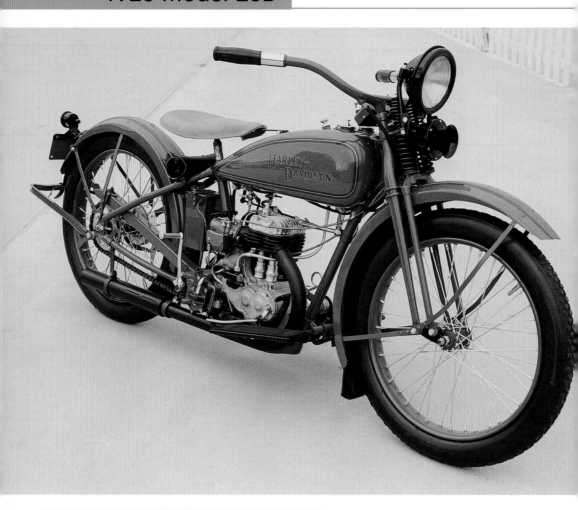

Year: 1926
Model: 26B
Engine: Single-cylinder, 21.35 cubic inches
Transmission: Three-speed
Features: Electric system

The 1926 Model B was less powerful, but also far less expensive, than other offerings from Harley.

Opposite: The stylish teardrop fuel tank lent an air of "big bike" to the smaller 26B, and helped drive people into the showrooms.

Harley-Davidson continued its efforts to regain market strength, offering several new models in 1926 that carried lower price tags along with their single-cylinder motors. New colors appeared for the entire lineup, though few buyers opted for them.

Of these new models, the 26B was powered by a 21.35-cubic-inch single-cylinder motor that was teamed up to a three-speed gearbox. The 26B was equipped with electric lighting, and a small rectangular panel on the handlebars held the pair of required keys. To further enhance buyers, the 26B sold for nearly $100 less than the twin-cylinder models of the same year. While delivering high fuel mileage, the 26B could also reach nearly 60 miles per hour, and was therefore considered well suited for everyday use.

Joined to a three-speed gearbox, the single-cylinder motor only displaced 21 cubic inches.

Although the new B models were racking up sales, the big JD remained Harley's best seller for 1927.

Year: 1927
Model: 27JD
Engine: Twin-cylinder,
    74 cubic inches
Transmission: Three-speed
Features: Electric lighting

Having introduced its new line of single-cylinder models the previous year, Harley-Davidson would have a fairly quiet year in 1927.

The twin-cylinder models now featured an ignition that lacked a distributor, curing the wet riding ills created by the former design. Both Harley and Indian had been frustrated by this ailment, and the new system corrected the trouble.

This would also be the final year for motor cases painted in the same olive green as the sheet metal. The new singles were selling fine, but the bigger 27JD rang up nearly 9,700 sales for the year, making it Harley's best selling 1927 model. The 1927 JD sold for $320, putting it at the top of the list prices for the year.

The big 74-inch V-twin was teamed up with a three-speed gearbox delivering plenty of power and ratios for any riding situation.

Also available as a 27JDS, the twin-cylinder machine was offered with sidecar gearing when plans were to add the passenger's throne.

A revised frame design placed the saddle and its rider two inches closer to the ground, making the 1930 models even easier to ride.

Lacking any clairvoyant powers, Harley-Davidson had penned sweeping changes for the 1929 and 1930 models. Sadly, the collapse of the stock market would bring the financial world to its knees only two months prior to the introduction of the latest models. The 1930 offerings were completely new and had been created prior to the crash of the financial markets.

Easily detachable wheels were added to the lineup and allowed for far easier changing of tires when troubles arose. Revised frames placed the riders closer to the riding surface while maintaining adequate ground clearance. The new Seventy-Four motors were a welcome change as was the far more powerful electric system which threw more light from the headlight.

A steering head lock was another new feature of the 1930 models and helped to thwart those who wanted to ride without buying.

For 1930, a 74-inch side-valve motor was introduced; it was a popular choice for those adding a sidecar to their Harley.

Year: 1930
Model: 30VS
Engine: Twin-cylinder, 74 cubic inches
Transmission: Three-speed
Features: Sidecar gearing

The VS model carried specific sidecar gearing within the transmission, making the machine more useful when moving three wheels down the road, regardless of which side of the bike the hack was mounted on.

Pressed into service by a North Carolina police force, the 1931 VL served the officer well with its high-compression 74-inch motor.

With most of the country still in the dark of the Depression, splashier graphics were used to lighten the spirits of potential buyers.

With an economy reeling from the effects of the Depression, and all new models being introduced the year before, 1931 would be another year without much fanfare for Harley.

Efforts to boost sales floor traffic included adding beautifully colored graphics to the fuel tanks of many models. Another change brought the single headlight back after the less than enthusiastic application of the dual-lamp setup.

Smaller alterations included cadmium plating on the brake lever and kick-starters, as well as vertically mounted generators. Die-cast Schebler carburetors fed the Forty-Five and Seventy-Four motors, delivering smoother flow of the fuel and air mixture. Additional variations of the V were also added to the roster to meet specific commercial demands.

Year: 1931
Model: 31D
Engine: Twin-cylinder, 45 cubic inches
Transmission: Three-speed
Features: Low-compression motor

The 1931 D model carried a 45-inch low-compression side-valve motor in the frame rails, along with a three-speed gearbox.

Despite the country being gripped by the Depression, the 1932 Harley catalog still carried 14 different models, including the V, the 74-inch medium-compression model.

Year: **1932**
Model: **32V**
Engine: **Twin-cylinder, 74 cubic inches**
Transmission: **Three-speed**
Features: **Medium-compression motor**

Helping to light the way at night, these accessory driving lamps mounted to a crossbar above the handlebars.

The trend for owners to accessorize their Harleys continued, as seen by the addition of a wicker basket and fire extinguisher.

The crushing effects of the Great Depression were felt keenly at all levels, and Harley-Davidson products were not singled out. Larger machines continued to sell poorly, so the Milwaukee builder reintroduced some smaller, less expensive machines to keep the assembly lines humming. The Twenty-One sold for a mere $195, but did little to boost overall production numbers.

Riding about midpack in the 1932 catalog, the 32V was fitted with a medium-compression 74-inch twin and a three-speed gearbox. Fuel strainers were added to the delivery line to keep unwanted detritus from reaching the carburetors, and the air intake pipe was lengthened. More generous spacing on the Seventy-Four's chain guards reduced the possibility of the drive chain getting wedged into the space.

1934 VLD models were a common choice among law enforcement agencies across the country.

Year: **1934**
Model: **34VLD**
Engine: **Twin-cylinder, 74 cubic inches**
Transmission: **Three-speed**
Features: **High-compression motor**

When sold for civilian use, the VLD often wore two-tone paint along with the 74-inch high-compression V-twin engine.

Continued use of colorful tank graphics added to the allure of the latest models in the Harley catalog.

Changes remained minimal for 1934, but extending the model year to include the entire calendar year allowed Harley-Davidson to tally some extra sales. This minor parlor trick, along with some trivial alterations, saw sales numbers reach 10,000, a far cry from the fewer than 4,000 seen in 1933.

Stronger frames and forks carried the revised front and rear fenders into the fray for 1934, producing the most graceful Harleys ever. A new Airflow taillight was mounted to the reshaped rear fender, bringing another touch of style to the table. Splashy tank graphics continued to be the flavor of the year as sales continued to sag during the Depression years. Of all models produced for 1934, the 34VLD tallied the most votes with just over 4,500 units being assembled.

1934 VLD models were a common choice among law enforcement agencies across the country.

Year: 1935
Model: 35VLD
Engine: Twin-cylinder 74 cubic inches
Transmission: Three-speed
Features: High-compression motor

When sold for civilian use, the VLD often wore two-tone paint along with the 74-inch high-compression V-twin engine.

Changes remained minimal for 1934, but extending the model year to include the entire calendar year allowed Harley-Davidson to tally some extra sales. This minor parlor trick, along with some trivial alterations, saw sales numbers reach 10,000, a far cry from the fewer than 4,000 seen in 1933.

Stronger frames and forks carried the revised front and rear fenders into the fray for 1934, producing the most graceful Harleys ever. A new Airflow taillight was mounted to the reshaped rear fender, bringing another touch of style to the table. Splashy tank graphics continued to be the flavor of the year as sales continued to sag during the Depression years. Of all models produced for 1934, the 34VLD tallied the most votes with just over 4,500 units being assembled.

Chapter Three: The Knucklehead's Debut

With the Great Depression beginning to fade, Harley could once again return to putting vast amounts of money into research and design. Even during the blight of the Depression, Harley forged ahead with new machines as they struggled to maintain equilibrium during a very challenging period. Changes came at a slower pace during the drought as did production numbers, but the assembly lines kept rolling, despite the drastically reduced output.

There was no question about the success of their chosen V-twin, 45-degree engine layout, so all they needed to do next was to enhance the performance of the concept. Most of the previous motors suffered from one type of lubrication woe or another and this concern was addressed vigorously by the R&D team in Milwaukee. Improved lubrication was joined by more efficient valve trains with the introduction of side-valve and overhead-valve motors introduced in 1926. Harley's first twin-cam model was seen in 1928 in the JDH. Although still an F-head motor, the addition of the second cam

boosted power. Fresh versions of the side-valve motor were seen in 1929 in the 30.50-inch single and 45-inch twin.

By 1930, the side- and overhead-valve motors had more than proven their worth, and the long-term F-head design was laid to rest. With financial restraints running strong, even Harley was forced to trim the fat from its lineup. The company chose to pursue newer technology despite the complaints heard from some F-head loyal buyers.

The latest iterations of flathead motors were joined by reconfigured chassis that provided more stability and comfort to the rider. Lower saddle heights were achieved as well, allowing more riders to comfortably maneuver their Harleys when parking. Experimentation with a dual-headlight arrangement ended in 1930, with Harley returning to the traditional single-lamp layout. The rattle-prone, fork-mounted tool boxes were also deleted from the bikes in the same year. Efforts to bring fresh buyers to the showrooms resulted in splashy graphic uses of color on the fuel tanks, making those machines easy to spot in the collector market today. The days of gray or olive green were long gone, with fanciful hues being applied to the revised sheet metal forms.

Continuing the styling trend in 1934, Harley installed shapely front and rear fenders to its machines bringing new levels of artistic expression to the catalog. Additionally, 1934 would also mark the final year of single-cylinder models being sold by Harley. With the market still stinging from the crash of the stock market, the few remaining buyers preferred the more powerful twins, making the decision an easy one for Harley management.

With only the twin-cylinder engines in its lineup, Harley continued to improve the output and efficiency of the layout. Conventional wisdom would have dictated using an existing motor and adding new hardware, but Harley chose to create something entirely new. In development for several years before making its debut as a 1936 model, the latest overhead valve motor would become an instant hit. The contours of the new rocker boxes earned the new motor the "Knucklehead" moniker, but the name had no adverse effect on sales of the freshly minted mills.

For its first several model years, the new Knucklehead engine experienced few engineering changes.

All new for the 1936 model year was the "Knucklehead"-powered EL, displacing 61 inches along with most of the competition.

The first 33 years of Harley-Davidson motorcycle history showed us the variety of ways a flathead, or F-head, motor could power a motorcycle. The format had proved itself to be both dependable and adaptable, but buyers demanded more power with less mess from their two-wheeled mounts.

Carried in the new double loop frames was the new overhead-valve motor that would come to be known as the "Knuckle-head" because of the contours of the valve covers. This brand new mill was fresh, from the cases up, and produced twice the power of the previous engine, but retained the same 61-cubic-inch displacement. Coupled to a four-speed gearbox, the new motor was smooth, and powerful, and it had a circulating lubrication system that kept things clean. Adding to the allure of the latest in technology were alterations in the styling of the 1936 models. A more streamlined fuel tank and fenders gave the machines a fresh profile that was instantly applauded by buyers.

The styling on the 1936 EL would set the standard for design in the United States, and was carried into future Harley-Davidson offerings.

Year: 1936
Model: EL
Engine: Twin-cylinder, 61 cubic inches
Transmission: Four-speed
Features: All new "Knucklehead" motor

Fresh styling accompanied the latest motor in the 1936 EL, and the tank top instrument panel was used for the first time ever.

With its debut in the previous year, the EL was seen with only minor changes on the 1937 models.

Year: 1937
Model: EL
Engine: Twin-cylinder, 61 cubic inches
Transmission: Four-speed
Features: High-compression motor

Opposite, top: Of the subtle alterations seen on the 1937s, the newly shaped air intake was one of the more obvious.

Opposite, bottom: Continued use of Harley-Davidsons in law enforcement agencies expanded as the latest machinery grew more powerful and dependable.

Incremental alterations appeared on the 1937 EL models, while the rest of the Harley catalog did its best to keep up. Far more changes were made to the remaining models than on the Knucklehead-powered versions, although the new ELs sported a revised air cleaner.

Improved manufacturing and assembly procedures allowed far more sharing of components among the Harley models. This level of interchangeable components placed the 61 OHV, Seventy-Four, and Eighty models into the "big twin" class with the Forty-Five carrying the balance. This blend of machines served the Milwaukee builder well, but the quickly approaching war would deliver sweeping changes to most of the product lines and their ultimate destination.

Although the new EL models grabbed most of the spotlight, Harley continued to sell flathead-powered machines, as seen in this 1937 ULH.

Year: 1937
Model: ULH
Engine: Twin-cylinder, 80 cubic inches
Transmission: Four-speed
Features: High-compression motor

The overall appearance of the ULH and other side-valve models was fairly close to the better-selling EL series.

For those buyers not willing to embrace the new overhead-valve models from Harley, a series of side-valve cycles were still sold alongside the Knuckleheads. The ULH featured an 80-inch displacement, high-compression engine, and a four-speed gearbox. Sharing many of the design details of the EL models, the ULH could be easily equipped with a wide variety of accessories directly from the local dealer.

Proof of the ULH's popularity was its ranking in the sales charts for 1937. The big side-valve model came in second and fell only a few hundred units short of meeting the EL in production.

Bright colors and highly stylized sheet metal are indicative of the late 1930s models from Harley, both the new EL and older side-valve models.

Even as the popularity of the latest EL grew, the tried and true side-valve models from Harley continued to be pressed into a variety of roles. Whether teamed with a sidecar for passenger use or mounted with a more utilitarian box, the 74-inch U proved vital to small business.

Used to ferry parts and supplies around town, this 1938 U is complete with a Package Delivery Car for the utmost in hauling capacity. With a lid that opens up fully, the rectangular space can be filled with any manner of materials required for a job or client. The powerful 80-inch motor provided ample horsepower for both the rider and his wares.

Carrying the rider, Package Delivery Car, and spare tire was no problem for the 1938 U, which also carried 74 inches of displacement in its side-valve motor.

Year: 1938
Model: U
Engine: Twin-cylinder, 74 cubic inches
Transmission: Four-speed
Features: Package Delivery Car,
    medium-compression motor

When equipped with either a sidecar or Package Delivery Car, the U was a well-balanced machine that was an economical option for small business.

Buyers continued to press their Harley-Davidsons into duty that exceeded carrying humans, as this 1938 U with the Package Delivery accessory demonstrates.

The 1939 EL was little changed from its previous variant, but was the best seller for that model year.

Year: **1939**
Model: **EL**
Engine: **Twin-cylinder, 61 cubic inches**
Transmission: **Four-speed**
Features: **High-compression motor**

Changes to the entire team of Harley-Davidson models continued to be subtle, while achieving higher levels of quality with every passing model year. The smaller Forty-Five-powered models gained features previously found on only the big twins, while those models also gained in dependability and performance. Late in 1939, Harley built and submitted for review a pair of Forty-Five models to the U.S. military.

Bearing only minor differences from its 1938 brother, the 1939 EL remained at the top of the sales charts. The 61-inch overhead-valve motor was proving to be everything the Motor Company had promised and more, and buyers were eager to bring one home.

Still displacing 61 inches, the EL motor was the catalyst that put the 1939 model at the top of the sales charts for Harley.

Two-tone paint schemes only added to the appeal of the EL model, and buyers had several hues from which to choose.

Building on the strong results posted by the 61-inch EL Knucklehead, an even bigger 74-inch FL was rolled out for 1941. People had come to love the enhancements the overhead-valve motor provided and, as always, wanted more power. The easiest way to increase output was to bump the displacement of the cylinders.

The boost in cubic inches delivered a horsepower rating of 48 at 5,000 rpm, whether the motor was the standard F or higher-compression FL version. The added power came at a price of $40 over the 61-inch EL in 1941.

Heavily accessorized, this 1941 EL is a prime example of what an owner could add to his Harley in the day.

Year: 1941
Model: EL and FL
Engine: Twin-cylinder, 61 cubic inches (EL), 74 cubic inches (FL)
Transmission: Four-speed
Features: High-compression motors

The bigger 74-inch motor was identical in outward dimensions, making it impossible to tell and EL from an FL.

The instrument panel on the 1941 models carried the set of "cat's eye" indicator lights that first appeared on the 1936 models.

Built to satisfy a government contract, the WLA was pressed into military service as World War II was taking hold of the planet.

Due to the war effort, 1942 saw a mix of civilian and military models, with production seriously skewed toward the latter. Many 1941 models were pulled from the catalog, and those that remained were only built in small numbers.

Of the three cycles built to meet with government contracts for the war effort, the WLA was produced in far greater numbers. Sold to the military only, the side-valve 45-inch motor was matched to a three-speed gearbox. It was employed in both combat and military base operations.

After their exposure to the WLA during World War II, many soldiers returning home bought surplus models and pressed them into civilian duty.

Equipped for service on the battlefield, the WLA carried a wide assortment of weapons and storage space, making sure the soldier had all he'd need.

Year: 1942
Model: WLA
Engine: Twin-cylinder, 45 cubic inches
Transmission: Three-speed
Features: Submachine gun scabbard,
        ammo boxes, heavy-duty luggage rack

While not as powerful as the bigger motors Harley built, the 45-inch side-valve provided adequate horsepower when pressed into battle.

Only 1,011 copies of the XA were built for military use, making them an unusual find today.

Year: 1942
Model: XA
Engine: Twin-cylinder, horizontally opposed, 45 cubic inches
Transmission: Four-speed
Features: Disc wheels, hydraulic suspension, opposed-cylinder motor

Fitted with heavy-duty suspension, solid wheels, and balloon tires, the XA was capable of overcoming almost any irregular surface.

The two cylinders of the XA's motor were horizontally opposed, and were mounted transversely in the chassis, unlike the 1919 Sport model Harley-Davidson once sold.

A new motor was developed for 1941 in response to the United States government's demand for a second military machine. The horizontally opposed configuration of the XA was loosely based on the time-tested layout used on BMW cycles, and displaced a little over 45 inches. Although the order to build 1,000 copies of this new bike was received in 1941, it would be listed as a 1942 model, due to the scheduled production dates.

The opposed cylinders of the XA's motor sent power to a four-speed gearbox, and the solid-disc wheels and oversized tires provided ample traction in uncertain terrain. Very few of the 1,011 XAs built made their way back to the States after the war, so finding a perfectly restored example is a rare sight.

With World War II over, buyers flocked to the showrooms, and the 61-inch EL was one of the bikes they rode home.

With World War II now receding into history, buyers found ways to satisfy their pent up demand for new products, including the need for two-wheeled fun. Many soldiers had been exposed to motorcycles for the first time during the war, and one of their first back-home purchases was a cycle of their own.

The 1947 Harleys wore a new taillight shape nicknamed the "tombstone," replacing the "beehive." With chrome plating returning to the fold, it was used on several parts, including the new tank badges. The speedometer was also revamped and now featured enhanced numerals and a red needle that indicated velocity.

To meet with the newfound demand, the Motor Company also added to its manufacturing space with the purchase of a new plant on Capitol Drive in Milwaukee. The war had curtailed racing activities, but eager riders of all experience levels were returning to the tracks and courses around the country. It wouldn't take long for the Harley-mounted riders to regain their prewar dominance aboard the latest hardware. Not one to rest on its laurels, Harley was already planning the next step, and 1947 would be the final year for the Knucklehead motors.

Year: 1947
Model: EL
Engine: Twin-cylinder, 61 cubic inches
Transmission: Four-speed
Features: High-compression motor

A revised "tombstone" taillight replaced the previous "beehive" unit.

Harley owners continued to find more ways to enjoy their two-wheeled toys, some even adding a third wheel and extra passenger capacity.

Chapter Four: The Panhead and More

The decision to eliminate single-cylinder machines, along with bringing out the much improved Knucklehead in 1936, resulted in amazing growth for the Motor Company. As with any company in the business of manufacturing, World War II took its toll on civilian production, but Harley soldiered through the war years and came out a strong contender. The same period of time found competitor Indian in poor health, with its expiration on the immediate horizon.

Racking up impressive numbers with the Knucklehead allowed Harley to maintain a high level of R&D even during the lean war years. The success of the battle-ready WLA model did nothing to hurt the bottom line either, and gave many inexperienced riders exposure to the world of motorcycles while serving their country. Upon their return home, many sought out a stateside machine to carry on their newfound interest in motorcycling. The availability of surplus WLAs made the introductory purchase almost painless for many, and led the way for Harley to continue improving the line.

Originally powered by a 61-cubic-inch motor, the EL was joined by a 74-inch variant named the FL in 1941. With two choices on the Knucklehead ballot, sales became more diverse, with law enforcement agencies scooping up the big twin models for official use. The ongoing war continued to sap the strength of civilian production, but buyers continued to bring home what they could from their local dealers.

In 1942, the WLA was produced in response to a large government contract, and the flathead model was joined by the opposed-twin XA in the same year. Nearly 80,000 copies of the WLA would be produced to fulfill the military's needs, while only 1,000 XAs were built in the same period. World War II would come to a close in 1945, allowing people to slowly get back to their normal lives. As with most industrial firms, Harley-Davidson would take a year or so to get its production back in line, and more changes were afoot for the legendary builder.

Clamoring to satisfy their pent-up desires for all things mechanical, buyers flocked to Harley dealers to get their hands on the 1947 models. The war effort had put the brakes on much in the way of major changes, so the 1947 lineup closely mirrored that of 1941. Among the incremental changes to the 1947 versions, a hydraulic damper was installed on the front forks, replacing the previously used friction style unit. The application of the small hydraulic item would foreshadow bigger changes soon to be employed by the engineers at Harley.

As they had done during the years of the Depression, Harley continued to revise their machines during the war. With the introduction of the EL in 1936, followed by the bigger FL in 1941, additional alterations were being crafted for the successful motor. Unlike the Knucklehead mill, the 1948 Panhead would be a combination of old and new. The bottom end of the 1948 motor would remain largely that of the 1936 design, but the aluminum-alloy cylinder heads were all new. Hydraulic lifters helped to quiet the motor's operation, along with delivering more efficient cooling. The latest motor weighed in at 8 pounds less than the Knucklehead it replaced, but provided no additional power. The progression into the alloy and hydraulic world would be seen as a great boon to the Harley catalog in the coming years, with every revision helping to fortify the Harley-Davidson reputation.

Police departments considered the big twins from Harley a perfect fit for their two-wheeled patrol vehicles.

The Panhead motor was Harley's latest big-twin powerplant and did well to keep the Milwaukee builder moving forward.

In 1948 Harley-Davidson introduced the Panhead, the latest iteration of the evolving V-twin motor. The years that followed would debut fresh models into the expanding roster.

Hoping to build on the success of the Knucklehead motor first sold in 1936, Harley kept some of that motor's functions intact while adding new technology to improve the breed. The lower end of the previous motor remained unchanged, but an all-new design was implemented into the cylinder heads.

Using aluminum alloy, the newest heads also featured aluminum-bronze valve seat inserts and steel valve guides. Hydraulic pushrod lifters were another first for the Milwaukee builder, and the all new configuration delivered more efficient cooling with less maintenance and a lower noise level. No gain in power was realized, but the new motor saved 8 pounds at weigh-in. Sold in both EL (61-inch) and FL (74-inch) versions, the new Panhead motor ushered in revised sales numbers of increasing volume.

By joining the lower end of the Knucklehead with improved alloy cylinder heads, the 1948 Panhead was born.

Year: 1948
Model: FL
Engine: Twin-cylinder, 74 cubic inches
Transmission: Four-speed
Features: New alloy cylinder heads

Retaining the classic lines of the previous models, the new FL was an improved version that carried Harley into the next two decades.

Joining the Harley team in 1948 was the diminutive S-125, bringing new riders into the showrooms.

Another new model in 1948 was the tiny S-125. Hoping to snare new buyers, Harley wanted a two-wheeled craft that was smaller and lighter to eliminate the "big bike" fears of some buyers. Powered by a 125-cc, single-cylinder motor, the S-125 promised high mileage and drew big numbers in the showrooms. More than 10,000 copies were produced in the first year.

A girder front fork added rigidity to the frame and gave the S-125 the look of a larger machine. The single-cylinder power-plant only produced around 2 horsepower, but it was enough to propel rider and machine along swiftly.

Displacing only 125 cc, the S-125's motor was hardly a powerhouse, but worked well enough to entice new buyers to the dealers.

Year: 1948
Model: S-125
Engine: Single-cylinder, 125 cc
Transmission: Three-speed
Features: Smaller size and price

Sharing the same tank badges as the full-sized models helped buyers to equate their smaller S-125s to the rest of the riders aboard the EL and FL models.

A pair of hydraulic front forks was installed on the 1949 big twin models, resulting in the birth of the Hydra-Glide name.

Year: 1949
Model: FL
Engine: Twin-cylinder, 74 cubic inch,
   high-compression
Transmission: Four-speed
Features: Hydra-Glide front suspension

Further enhancement of the Panhead models came in 1949 with the installation of hydraulic front forks. The vastly improved suspension, tagged Hydra-Glide by the Motor Company, smoothed out the ride of the big twins. The older version of the front fork could still be had, but most buyers opted for the latest technology.

The E and F variants still offered the buyer a selection of compression and gearing to more specifically meet with the intended use of the machine. The high-compression 74-inch FL was the most popular model for 1949, with just over 8,000 copies being shipped to dealers.

The Panhead motor was trimmed with a wide array of gleaming stainless steel bits for 1949, including the available air cleaner cover.

Businesses continued to put their Harley-Davidsons to work, as witnessed by the installation of the package delivery car on this 1949 FL.

Only minor changes graced the 1952 FL, but the big twin machine continued to sell well.

The year 1952 was another marked by new models appearing and some familiar faces fading away. Of those passing names, the WL, which had been around since 1937 and had served well, phased out of production. Replacing it was the brand new K model. Motivated by a 45-inch side-valve motor, complete with alloy cylinder heads, the K also rode on hydraulic suspension at both ends, something the big twins wouldn't see until 1958. Taking performance to the next level, the KR and KRTT machines began strafing tracks across the country with amazing success.

On the EL and FL models, the more modern hand-clutch, foot-shift variants were offered, but some of the died-in-the-wool crowd still liked the original method of shifting gears. A spring-loaded aid for the new foot shifter earned the nickname "mousetrap," but it did assist in the chore of selecting gears. Also, 1952 was the last year for the smaller 61-inch EL models, as buyers chose the bigger FL model at a rate of almost three to one.

Year: 1952
Model: FL
Engine: Twin-cylinder, 74 cubic inches
Transmission: Four-speed
Features: Color-matched grips and pedal

First used on the 1951 models, the scripted logo returned for another year in 1952.

Finished in Persian Red, this 1952 FL also has the matching hand grips and kick-start pedal.

Several two-tone paint options were available for the 1954 models as well, adding some variation to the lineup.

The strength and dependability of the big twin models found them being used on a large number of law enforcement agencies across the United States.

Harley-Davidsons would be adorned with 50th Anniversary badges to commemorate the maker's birthday in 1954. Although the company began in 1903, actual "production" hadn't been claimed until 1904, thus the shift in the birthday. Along with the birthday badges, a few alterations were made to the latest Milwaukee machines.

In the trim division, a new Jubilee horn was added to most models, replacing the less ornate circular version. For the first time, every 74-inch model could be ordered wearing a set of two-tone sheet metal. The smaller 61-inch E models had seen their last days, as the resounding popularity of the bigger motor won out.

The 1954 models bore several 50th anniversary badges. This FL also wears the color-keyed hand grips.

Year: 1954
Model: FL
Engine: Twin-cylinder, 74 cubic inches
Transmission: Four-speed
Features: Available two-tone sheet
  metal

Highly accessorized, this 1955 FLF sports the hard-sided saddlebags along with nearly every optional bit of chrome and trim.

Changes to the FL models in 1955 were minor, with most aimed at improving the motor's service needs. The inlet manifold was now connected to the cylinders using O-rings and hose clamps, making access a lot easier.

The previous FLH designation was added to the roster, with the FLH moniker being applied to the higher compression model. The FLF was still the foot-shift version while the FL retained the hand-shift operation. The FLE was the Traffic Model.

Revisions to the tail light and chrome fork surround were about the only real cosmetic issues found on the FL line. Another new tank logo was also installed across the model line.

Above: The 50th Anniversary badges remained in place on the front fenders, although the official birthday had fallen in 1954.

Above, left: The tank-mounted instrument panel was still in use, but now lacked the famous "cat eyes" warning lamps.

Year: 1955
Model: FLF
Engine: Twin-cylinder, 74 cubic inches
Transmission: Four-speed
Features: Foot-shift

The higher-powered KHK, first sold as a 1955 model, would make its last appearance in 1956.

A swooping graphic panel was seen on all the 1956 models, along with the latest badge that was introduced on the 1955s.

The 55-inch motor used in the K and KHK had been a vast improvement over the previous mill, but was to be replaced in 1957.

The K model was first sold as a 1952 model and was powered by a 45-inch side-valve motor with alloy heads. The K was then updated to become the KH in 1954 and carried a 55-inch motor. The high performance KHK rolled onto showroom floors in time for the 1955 model year, and was again revised for 1956.

A modified frame now had the rider seated lower to the ground while the 55-inch side-valve motor was still in use. It was another smaller Harley that came equipped with front and rear suspension a full six years ahead of the FL models.

Year: 1956
Model: KHK
Engine: Twin-cylinder, 55 cubic inches, side-valve
Transmission: Four-speed
Features: High performance version of the KH

The KH and KHK variants would make their final appearance in 1956, as Harley prepared the rollout of their next all new machine for 1957.

Replacing the short-lived K models, the XL family was introduced for 1957 and continues to be sold to this day.

Year: 1957
Model: XL
Engine: Twin-cylinder, 55 cubic inches,
　　　overhead valves
Transmission: Four-speed
Features: Aluminum pistons, hemispherical heads

Right: The "Sportster" name was cast into the left-hand engine case, making a bold statement for the smaller Harley.

Following on the heels of a few lackluster years, 1957 would see a fresh face on the bench as Harley continued its efforts to lure new buyers into the showrooms. The K model and its variants had proven themselves to be a good draw for buyers of a smaller Harley, but the new-for-1957 XL would take the K model's place. The motor was all new, rather than a melding of K and FL components. Aluminum pistons slid inside the cast-iron jugs, topped with hemispherical heads. Overhead valves delivered better performance than the side-valve KH and ushered in a new era for Harley. The four-speed gearbox was shifted with a foot lever found on the right side of the chassis, a feature typically seen on British made models. The XL sold fairly well in its first year, and additional iterations would boost those numbers higher in the coming years.

The 55-inch motor used in the XL model was all new, and not a combination of any previous mills from Harley.

Very few alterations were made to the big FL models for 1957, but they continued to be a favorite of buyers. Steel alloy valve guides were added to the motor's top end, and heavier valve springs were added to the recipe by model year end. A fresh speedometer face was also seen on the 1957 FL models, along with a one-year-only tank badge design.

The FLHF was Harley-Davidson's top seller in 1957, racking up a total of 2,614 units produced.

Year: 1957
Model: FLHF
Engine: Twin-cylinder, 74 cubic inches, high-compression
Transmission: Four-speed
Features: Foot-shift model

A revised tank badge was applied to the 1957 models, along with another variation in the paint scheme.

Left: Owners continued to add accessories to their Harley-Davidsons for 1957, making each example a personal statement.

Heralding the debut of hydraulic suspension at both ends, the 1958 Duo-Glide was a great leap forward.

New for 1958 were the Duo-Glide models featuring hydraulic suspension at both ends of the big twin chassis. Along with the hydraulic rear shocks, a brake of the same design was added to the rear wheel, helping to slow the big machines in record time.

Duo-Glide badges were found on each side of the front fender, heralding the new design. A set of S-shaped fender braces were also added to comply with the newfound motion at the rear end. This bit of hardware remains in use today on Harley-Davidsons.

A two-into-one exhaust was stock, but an owner could easily change that to a two-into-two arrangement by purchasing the required hardware. The FLHF was again found at the top of the sales charts, ringing in just under 3,000 sales for the model year.

Year: 1958
Model: FLHF
Engine: Twin-cylinder, 74 cubic inches
Transmission: Four-speed
Features: Hydraulic suspension on
   rear wheel

Well dressed in their
gleaming chrome housings,
a set of hydraulic shocks
brings a new level of
comfort to the Harley rider.

The Duo-Glide name was
proudly applied to the front
fenders of Harley's latest big
twin models.

Dubbed the XLCH, this 1958 model was built for speed; it lacked any form of lighting, and was delivered in this race-ready form.

Year: **1958**
Model: **XLCH**
Engine: **Twin-cylinder, 55 cubic inches, overhead valves**
Transmission: **Four-speed**
Features: **No lighting, shorty exhaust pipes**

The oil tank of the XLCH wore a special decal that advertised the bike's potential.

With 55 inches pounding in the walls of the cylinders and truncated exhaust pipes, the checkered flag tank graphics seemed redundant.

Three new XL variants were created: the XLH, XLC, and XLCH. Each carried a different set of hardware catering to a specific clientele. The XLC and XLCH were the performance birds in the nest, wearing no lighting and sporting truncated rear fenders for a truly aggressive appearance. Stubby exhaust pipes did little to dispel the nature of these models, nor did they do much to quiet the departing exhaust note.

A high-compression version of the same 55-inch overhead-valve motor was used in the XLCH, earning it the "XL, Competition Hot" moniker. Due to the sporting nature of the XLCH, only 239 examples of the 1958 version were produced that year.

Seen here in Hi-Fi Green and Birch White, this 1960 FLHF also sports a number of period accessories.

Another year of subtle revisions marked the 1960 lineup, especially in the FL family. New paint and graphics made the latest versions easy to spot, while the internal changes went unnoticed.

The chrome nacelle that surrounded the headlight was now a two-piece affair, as well as the handlebars, which were joined by a central clamp.

Previously used only on the FLH models, Stellite-faced valves were now installed on the FL models. Revised oil-control piston rings were joined by an even heavier set of valve springs.

The 1960 FLHF sold for $1,375, and was second in price to only the Servi-Car models.

A popular item since its inception, the tank-mounted dash remained for the 1960 models.

The two-tone spark plug wraps are seen here, along with the infamous "mouse-trap" spring-loaded clutch assist device.

Year: 1960
Model: FLHF
Engine: Twin-cylinder, 74 cubic inches
Transmission: Four-speed
Features: High-compression motor, foot-shift

New tank graphics and a high level of added trim make this 1961 FLF a stand-out example.

Year: 1961
Model: FLH
Engine: Twin-cylinder, 74 cubic inches
Transmission: Four-speed
Features: New paint and badges for 1961

Revised again for 1961, the tank stripes make it easy to spot models of that model year.

The ongoing success of the FL line allowed Harley-Davidson to leave the models mostly untouched for 1961. But, as always, they implemented some changes to further the cause. Replacing the sometimes-erratic wasted-spark ignition was a dual-points, dual-fire system that delivered a stronger and more dependable spark. Yet another version of the cast tank badges was found on the 1961 FLH, along with an altered paint scheme and revised "FLH" appliqués on the oil tank. This example was finished in Hi-Fi Red with Birch White trim, and was a common choice of period buyers.

The price of the 1961 FLH climbed $25 over the previous year, and the company was beginning to feel the heat from the newly minted Asian imports that were reaching the shores of the United States.

Yet another variation in the paint and stripe theme was applied to the 1963 models, and add-on trim abounded.

Year: 1963
Model: FLHF
Engine: Twin-cylinder, 74 cubic inches
Transmission: Four-speed
Features: High-compression, foot-shift

Above: Additional application of chrome trim was becoming quite common, as owners did their best to make a statement with their new Harleys.

Upper left: Heavy application of chrome trim can be found on this 1963 FL model and is fairly typical for the period.

The FLHF had proven its mettle by remaining at the top of the production number charts for many years, and 1963 would be no different. Continuous improvement kept the big FL headed in the right direction, as service and comfort issues were addressed.

Oil lines for the 74-inch motor were once again running on the outside of the powerplant instead of the inner mounting started during the Knucklehead period. The rear drum brake could now be relined instead of simply replaced when it was time to be serviced.

In the cosmetics department, "fishtail" muffler tips were all the rage and could be purchased new from your local Harley dealer along with the optional dual-exhaust. Another version of the cast tank badge was employed on the 1963 models along with yet another variation in the paint stylings.

With the exception of the fresh tank paint arrangement, little else was altered on the 1964 XLCH.

Only two versions of the XL model remained in the 1964 catalog, with the XLCH listed as the top model. Both variants received a full-width, aluminum front brake drum, which enhanced the XLCH's stopping power immensely.

The previously black lower fork bracket was supplanted with a chrome version to brighten up the overall appearance. Inside the motor, aluminum tappets were used, and a better clutch seal was achieved through the use of a polyacrylic material. Birch White side panels graced the XLCH's fuel tank, and were also found on most of the Harley-Davidson 1964 lineup.

The motor of the XLCH soldiered on with no changes for the latest year of production.

Year: 1964
Model: XLCH
Engine: Twin-cylinder, 55 cubic inches
Transmission: Four-speed
Features: Aluminum front drum brake

Rear shocks on the XLCH were tucked inside the chrome towers that were bolted to each side of the chassis.

Year: **1964**

Model: **FLHF**

Engine: **Twin-cylinder, 74 cubic inches**

Transmission: **Four-speed**

Features: **Two-key system**

Above: Finished in Hi-Fi Blue and Birch White, this 1964 FLH is fitted with the matching windshield, adding more comfort to the equation.

Opposite: When equipped with the two-person buddy seat, windshield, and chrome trim, the FLHF was ready for anything.

As 1964 was the penultimate year of the Panhead motor used in the FL line, changes to the model were minimal at best. With sales strong as always, Harley made more evolutionary changes versus radical alterations during its span.

The latest FL was now parked on a wider Jiffy stand, and the oil pressure switch was enhanced. Late in the model year, a two-piece chain guard was added to the mix. Motorcycle theft was growing as fast as the industry, and the 1964 FLs used a two-key system to thwart an easy steal. One key released the fork lock, while the second was used to start the bike.

White side panels on the fuel tanks were also used on the FL in 1964, adding continuity to the line's design theme.

While 1965 would usher in the era of the electric start models, it was the final year for the Panhead motor.

Year: **1965**
Model: **FLFB**
Engine: **Twin-cylinder, 74 cubic inches**
Transmission: **Four-speed**
Features: **First year for Electra Glide, last year for Panhead motor**

Until the 1965 models were introduced, every Harley on the showroom floor was started using a kick pedal and the power in your leg. Debuting in 1965, the Electra Glide was a big twin model that was also fitted with an electric start. Only the touch of a button was required to bring the 74-inch FL motors to life, adding a new level of convenience to the equation. Production of the newly minted craft nearly doubled for the latest model year, proving the value of the electric start entries. Sold in four variations, the freshest revision to the Harley stable was well received. This feature was only added to the FL line for now, but would later be seen on every machine that Harley produced.

The Motor Company was laying the groundwork for the next iteration of its popular V-twin powerplant, and 1965 would play out as the final year for the Panhead motor. Even the installation of the electric start would do little to protect Harley from the influx of Japanese-built machines that were flowing into the country.

A large chrome battery box concealed the 12-volt system used to start the Electra Glide. The old fashioned kick-start pedal remained as a back-up.

The Electra Glides were also given the revised alpha moniker of FLB models for 1965, setting them apart from the previous FLH-designated models.

Chapter Five: The Shovelhead Years

With the introduction of the 1948 Panhead-powered models, Harley's success continued to swell. Civilian riders, as well as the growing applications by law enforcement, proved that the Motor Company was on the right track. Not only were their machines improving, but effective management was keeping things on the right path.

Building on the success of the latest motor, 1949 saw the introduction of a hydraulic front fork, creating the Hydra-Glide moniker. This advance in suspension design brought an entirely new cadre of riders to the fold, along with impressing the die-hard Harley fans. For the truly hard-core buyers, the older front fork could still be had on the 1949 big twins, but only until the 1950 catalog arrived. Time marched on, and in its wake certain features were simply put out to pasture.

Along with changes to the existing big twin models, other models were added and weaned from the team. The WL was no longer offered as part of the 1952 model lineup, but another small machine would enter the fray. The K models were propelled by a 45-inch side-valve motor that was built with alloy heads. The smaller machine was designed to draw buyers to the showrooms that were resistant to riding the massive big twin variants. For the first time on a Harley, the K also rode on hydraulic suspension at both ends. This feature was to precede the application of rear shocks on the Panhead by six years. The new K model also carried a retail price that was about $100 less than the big twin, which was a needed incentive for some buyers.

Harley's rival, Indian, made its final sales in 1953, leaving Harley as the only U.S. manufacturer of motorcycles. It had been 50 years earlier that Harley built its first machine, but the official 50th anniversary would not be marked until the 1954 models were introduced.

Another new model was introduced in 1957, taking the place of the short-lived K and its variants. The XL, or Sportster, featured much of the same engineering used on the previous K, but was driven by a more powerful motor. Side-stepping the use of old and new, the XL was fitted with yet another fresh motor. The fabled 45-degree

V-twin configuration bristled with new technology. Aluminum pistons rode in cast-iron walls, and hemispherical heads were bolted to the top. Aluminum alloy was also employed in the pushrods and rocker boxes to save weight.

Big twin models for 1959 finally found hydraulic suspension at both ends of their chassis, bringing another measure of comfort to the rider. Joining the cadre of evolutionary alterations during its life span, the Panhead would be fitted with an electric start in 1965. No longer forced to kick-start the booming V-twin to life, a simple push of a button achieved the same goal. This feature proved to be a real lifesaver at a time when Harley-Davidson was beginning to feel the heat from Asian models being imported into the United States.

Following the introduction of the push-button start on the Electra Glide, Harley brought out the latest iteration of their V-twin, which would become known as the Shovelhead. Bolting new "power pac" aluminum heads to the lower end of the Panhead gained a 10 percent boost in horsepower along with quieter operation. The introduction of the new motor bumped numbers on the sales floor too, adding 1,000 units to the total sold over the previous year's models.

Even the fresh motor would do little to protect Harley from the onslaught of incoming Japanese machines, and 1969 would provide a painful lesson as Honda debuted its CB750 to the U.S. market. The Motor Company would need to do a lot more than bolt on new heads to survive the next round.

The XR-750 had become a dominant factor in the racing world soon after its debut in 1969, and it remained one in 1975.

Equipped with the latest Shovelhead engine, electric start, and a full complement of accessories, the 1966 FLH is ready for anything.

With the exception of the new Shovelhead motor, the big FL models were basically unchanged from the Panheads they replaced.

Harley-Davidson, a dominant industry player since the creation of the firm in 1903, was now feeling the pressure Asian imports were applying. Relying heavily on its existing hardware and core audience, Harley forged ahead with a new motor to accompany the latest electric start option that had appeared in 1965.

Continuing to build on the success of the Panhead motor, Harley simply adapted a fresh set of cylinder heads to the existing lower end, creating the Shovelhead. Named for the curving shape of the aluminum heads, the new motor produced 10 percent more power and ran more quietly. A Linkert Model

DC carburetor was also installed to better monitor the flow of fuel and air, bringing the level of performance up another notch. Upon their arrival at the local dealers, the newest FLB and FLHB models flew out the door. Even the influx of Japanese machinery was not enough to keep buyers away from the storied brand and its iconic motorcycles.

Year: 1966
Model: FLHFB
Engine: Twin-cylinder, 74 cubic inches
Transmission: Four-speed
Features: New Shovelhead motor

When set up with the hard-sided saddlebags, windshield, and buddy seat, a couple could easily spend the weekend traveling on their Shovelhead-powered Electra Glide.

Another of Harley's fearsome race machines, this KR750TT was ridden by Bart Markel.

Year: 1967
Model: KR750TT
Engine: Twin-cylinder, 45 cubic inches
Transmission: Four-speed
Features: Purpose-built race motorcycle

Harley-Davidson machines continued to dominate in certain forms of racing, especially when piloted by one of their legendary riders. Bart Markel was one such rider, and when aboard his 1967 KR750TT there were few that could rival his talents.

The 45-inch motor was built for competition use only. It exhaled through a set of proper race pipes, which provided very little in the way of sound reduction. As a race machine, the TT was devoid of any electrics or excess trim. The rigid chassis also held a four-speed gearbox in check, providing a visit for Bart and many others to victory circle on a regular basis.

The simple combination of power, handling, and light weight was nearly unbeatable, especially when in capable hands.

The 45-inch motor was coupled to a four-speed gearbox and proved to be a winning mixture.

The 1968 XLCH remained a top seller and performer for Harley, even as competition was making its way from across the pond.

Year: **1968**
Model: **XLCH**
Engine: **Twin-cylinder, overhead-valve, 55 cubic inches**
Transmission: **Four-speed**
Features: **Improved front forks**

The most dramatic change for 1968 would be the addition of a new corporate partner in AMF. After their years of being the top dog, Harley found itself holding on to market share and losing sales at a rapid clip to the Japanese cycles now being sold on U.S. shores. The deep pockets of AMF were at first seen to be a saving grace, but appearances can be deceiving.

Improvements on the 1968 XLCH and XLH were minimal, but included revised fork damping and additional travel. The XLH lost its kick-start pedal and could be ordered with the smaller peanut tank used on the XLCH. The XLCH was still Harley's second-best selling model despite its smaller size.

A chrome luggage rack added a touch of utility to the XLCH, but performance was still its strong suit.

Of the two Sportsters offered for the 1970 model year, the XLH ranked second to its higher performance XLCH kin.

Emblazoned with the "H" decal on the oil tank, there was no mistaking the intentions of the XLH Sportster.

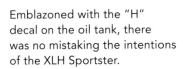

The XLH was often put into action as a touring mount, as witnessed by this well-equipped 1970 model.

Now fully ensconced with their new corporate partner, Harley-Davidson pressed on with changes across the board on the 1970 models. The XLH got a revised ignition that included points and a coil. The generator that had been employed on earlier editions was eliminated from the build sheet.

The 1970 buyer also had the option of adding Harley's latest styling trick, a fiberglass "boat tail" rear fender assembly. The option was not wildly accepted, but would not be eliminated for another year.

Year: 1970
Model: XLH
Engine: Twin-cylinder, 55 cubic inches
Transmission: Four-speed
Features: Optional boat tail rear fender

New for 1971 was the FX, which combined the FL frame and more nimble XL suspension.

With a gap between the smaller XL models and the larger FLBs, Harley announced the all new FX series for 1971. By joining the frame of the FL with the suspension of the XL, Harley hoped that the latest entry would appeal to a wider audience. The unusual boat tail rear fender that was first seen on the 1970 Sportsters was also installed on the FX. While the styling was certainly different, people were not wild about the design. It did however make a bold statement that Harley-Davidson was willing to take a chance from time-to-time, departing from their more traditional styling.

The new Super Glide weighed 70 pounds less than the big FL, allowing the FX to deliver more potent acceleration from the same 74-inch Shovelhead motor.

118

The unusual rear fender option was still available on the 1971 XLH, as seen in this example.

First sold as an option on the 1970 Sportsters, the fiberglass tail section was applied to the new FX as well.

Year: 1971
Model: FX Super Glide
Engine: Twin-cylinder, 74 cubic inches
Transmission: Four-speed
Features: Boat tail rear fender, optional "Sparkling America" paint

Designed for the smaller rider, the 1972 Shortster allowed younger riders to join in on the two-wheeled fun.

Year: 1972
Model: MC Shortster
Engine: Single-cylinder, 65 cc, two-stroke
Transmission: Three-speed
Features: Small size, ease of operation

Although it lacked in the way of many creature comforts, the Shortster made a terrific platform for the younger rider to learn the ropes of two-wheeled fun.

The 65-cc Shortster arrived for 1972 and drew the applause of younger riders who wanted a set of wheels they could call their own. Additional improvements were made to nearly every model as the company continued to fend off competition from the overseas manufacturers.

Using a two-stroke, single-cylinder motor that was mated to a three-speed gearbox, the Shortster offered plenty of fun for the smaller rider. The motor was another taken from Harley-Davidson's venture with the Aermacchi firm, and the little MC sold fairly well in its first year.

A pair of disc brakes helped to slow the 1973 FL models and was a welcome addition to the heavyweight machine.

A set of horizontal bars adorned the tank of the 1973 FL and accented the purple paint nicely.

Changes to the big FL models for 1973 were numerous. A second disc brake was added to the layout, providing better braking at both axles. The optional hand shift models were pulled from the catalog, forcing all riders to now shift with their boot. The advent of electric starting had made the kick-start pedal redundant since 1965, and it was finally removed from the machines in 1973.

The FL only came in two flavors for 1973, and neither model was seen at the top of the production charts, as smaller cycles gained favor.

The big FL could still haul a variety of rider, passenger, and luggage with ease despite its bulk.

Year: 1973
Model: FL
Engine: Twin-cylinder, 74 cubic inches
Transmission: Four-speed
Features: Second disc brake

Hoping to draw even larger groups of riders into the Harley-Davidson fold, the Motor Company continued to explore the options offered by smaller, more nimble machines.

The SS-250 was a larger version of the earlier SS-175 and was meant for use on the street. For those wanting on- and off-road capabilities, the SX-250 was at their avail.

The two-stroke motor displaced 250 cc, and rowed through a five-speed gearbox for maximum flexibility and eager response. Not a huge hit in its first year, the SS-250 still filled the needs of many riders.

Created for on-road use, the 1975 SS-250 was a fresh face in the Harley family portrait.

Year: 1975
Model: SS-250
Engine: Single-cylinder, 250 cc, two-stroke
Transmission: Five-speed
Features: Two person saddle, five-speed gearbox

The single cylinder, 250-cc motor was mated to a five-speed gearbox, providing plenty of options.

While powered by an Italian motor, the SS-250 was still an American-made machine, and the side covers showed the world.

The XLCR was a menacing design, cloaked in black and utilizing several unique features in its 1977 debut.

Several new models were added in 1977, and many changes were being made to those that still remained.

Flying in the face of convention, the XLCR rolled into the showrooms wearing an all-black motif, along with a bikini fairing and cast wheels. A 61-inch motor exhaled through a unique set of siamesed exhaust pipes, also finished in black. Die-cast wheels in matching black with polished highlights continued the theme; and a black seat, fuel tank, and tail section were all seen only on the XLCR.

This factory custom would not sell well at first, but would become a coveted model in later years.

From the bikini fairing to the sleek tail section, the XLCR was a fresh look at what a factory Harley could be.

Year: 1977
Model: XLCR
Engine: Twin-cylinder, 61 cubic inches
Transmission: Four-speed
Features: All-black motif, siamesed
    exhaust

One of the more distinctive features on the 1977 XLCR was the siamesed exhaust system that carried spent fumes away from the 1,000-cc motor.

Year: **1977**
Model: **MX250**
Engine: **Single-cylinder, 249 cc,
    two-stroke**
Transmission: **Five-Speed**
Features: **Light weight, ground
    clearance, suspension travel**

First sold to the public as a 1977 model, the MX250 was crafted to take on the motocross series, which was gaining in popularity.

Opposite: Built to meet with typical needs of the motocross rider, ground clearance was huge and the machine was light in weight.

Seeing a growing interest in the now AMA-sanctioned motocross class, Harley-Davidson decided to throw its helmet into the ring. A hundred copies of the MX250 were built and tested in 1976 before hitting the showrooms in 1977.

Powered by a 249-cc, two-stroke motor built by Harley's Italian partners at Aermacchi, the MX250 did an admirable job of flinging the dirt. Weighing in at only 233 pounds, the MX250 possessed quick handling.

Sadly for Harley, the influx of Japanese motorcycles was not limited to street models, and the selection, price, and features made them far more popular than the MX, which would only exist for two model years before being retired.

Displacing 249 cc in a two-stroke configuration, the MX250 motor produced ample power, but the model was soon left in the dirt by Asian imports.

The XR-750 continued to be a strong contender at racing venues in 1977.

After nearly a decade, the XR-750 remained a strong contender on racing circuits around the country. Initially built to attack flat-track venues, the XR-750 would be utilized in a variety of racing through the years.

Even the onslaught of Japanese machinery had a tough time overcoming the talents of the XR-750, mainly in part to its low weight and terrific power. Eventually, the duty of the legendary XR-750 was eclipsed by more modern equipment, but the history books would forever carry the name in their pages.

Year: 1977
Model: XR-750
Engine: Twin-cylinder, 45 cubic inches
Transmission: Four-speed
Features: 90 horsepower, 300-pound weight

Displacing only 45 cubic inches, the motor of the XR-750 could hammer out 90 horsepower, moving the 300-pound cycle along swiftly.

The rear end of the XR-750 was the sight seen most often by competitors as the mighty machine roared into the lead and stayed there.

A strong seller in 1977, its first year, the FXS Low Rider was what Harley buyers had been asking for, and the 1978 models were even more popular.

Year: 1978
Model: FXS Low Rider
Engine: Twin-cylinder, 74 cubic inches
Transmission: Four-speed
**Features: Low saddle height, flat
   handlebars, cast wheels**

First rolled out as a 1977 model, the FXS Low Rider, had turned out to be a crowd favorite among Harley buyers. The low-slung saddle, flat drag-bars, and cast wheels formed the perfect combination of style and function, and it would become the second-most produced model for 1978.

While the 1977 editions were sold in only the gray paint with red tank trim, the 1978s could be had with a contrasting two-tone scheme of black and silver. Improvements to the valve train were implemented in the middle of 1978 production.

Buyers loved the style and function of the Low Rider, and its appearance didn't hurt sales either.

The 1978 XL1000 was an anniversary model and was trimmed accordingly.

Seventy-five years of uninterrupted production were marked in 1978, and several birthday editions were sold to commemorate the anniversary. Of these bikes, the XL1000 was trimmed with gold and had a saddle uphol-stered in leather.

Year: 1978
Model: XLH Anniversary Edition
Engine: Twin-cylinder, 61 cubic inches
Transmission: Four-speed
Features: Black and gold paint, gold colored wheels, leather saddle

Gold trim, leather saddle, and gleaming black paint help the Anniversary Edition of the 1978 XLH stand out from a crowd.

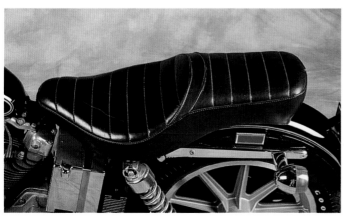

A leather saddle and gold wheels helped to set this XL1000 apart from other models sold that year.

Rolling into view for the first time as a 1980 model, the FLT returned in 1981 powered by the 80-inch Shovelhead motor.

The entire line of Harley motorcycles, including the new FLT, received an improved electronic ignition. The big twin model was built on an all-new frame that included compressible motor mounts to reduce vibration felt by the rider. A frame-mounted fairing held a pair of round headlights behind the domed cover. The new FLT weighed in at 725 pounds before fluids were added.

In 1981, the Motor Company was sold back to those who truly cared about the product, not just producing as many units as possible. Not only did the management team remove AMF from the letterhead, but also pulled the 74-inch Shovelhead motor from the option sheet. The bigger 80-inch mill had been grabbing most of the sales anyway, so few cries were heard at the loss of the smaller version.

The Shovelhead motor was fitted with an exhaust that crossed over to the right side of the chassis in two-into-two style.

Proudly emblazoned with eagle trim, the FLT claimed Harley's American heritage.

Year: 1981
Model: FLT
Engine: Twin-cylinder, 80 cubic inches
Transmission: Four-speed
Features: Frame-mounted fairing, new 80-inch motor

The blacked-out Sturgis model was also called the FXB; it featured a drive belt along with red trim.

Year: 1982
Model: FXB Sturgis
Engine: Twin-cylinder, 80 cubic inches
Transmission: Four-speed
Features: Black and red motif, last year of sale

The last year for the Sturgis edition was 1982, but later examples would be seen from Harley.

Creating a special model to commemorate the annual pilgrimage to the Black Hills in South Dakota, the FXB Sturgis served the Motor Company well. The classic black paint with red trim seemed timeless and a perfect tip of the hat to the rally.

The dual-belt design was still in use on the 1982 models, and had proven itself a durable option to the chain drive still in use on most other motorcycles.

All good things must end, and 1982 was to be the final year for the FXB Sturgis model. Not gone forever, it would reappear in the 1990s.

Chapter Six: Enter the EVO

It had been more than 80 years since the small group of Milwaukee builders painted "Harley-Davidson" on the side of their first machine, and the Motor Company had survived a long list of disasters as they marched forward. For the most part they stayed the course when it came to the design of their legendary V-twin motors, although several iterations had been sold throughout their history. While a few examples of other configurations made their way into the sales catalogs, the heart of a true Harley-Davidson would always be the 45-degree V-twin. The Shovelhead had been an improvement over the Panhead it replaced, but it was time for Harley to make a radical change if they were to not only continue to survive, but expand their reach in the market.

Seeing no need to reinvent the wheel, Harley simply applied their tried and true configuration while applying the most modern technology to the formula. The result of this mixture would be the V2 Evolution, or "Evo" motor. The latest iteration of the classic V-twin mill was assembled using a myriad of fresh materials and revised thinking. They needed a motor that would cure the ills of any past effort and push the company into the coming years. Alloy cylinders wore inner sleeves of iron for durability while the newly designed heads made the best use of the lower octane fuels found in most locations. A displacement of 80 inches was the only size offered for the new motor. All of this free flowing mixture was fired by a hotter spark, provided by a much-improved electronic ignition. The shape of the new cylinder heads would earn the new motor the "Blockhead" nickname, but "Evo" was used with equal ease.

With the new motor in their portfolio, Harley-Davidson set out to create some new excitement for the line. The first year for the Evo was 1984, but not every machine would carry it. The Sportster models would retain the Shovelhead mill for another two years, and the FLH and FLHX also kept the Shovelhead for a final year. The FXE, FXSB, and FXWG would find the older motor in their frames for the first part of the production period with the new V2 motor being slipped in later.

Another change to the 1984 catalog was the appearance of the Softail models. Early examples of Harley-Davidsons lacked any form of rear suspension, and some modern buyers liked the cleaner look of that design. While they liked the look, they still wanted a soft ride, thus creating the need for a hidden suspension system. A pair of reclusive shocks rode under the frame rails, hidden from view while providing ample suspension travel at the rear wheel. The melding of old and new reached a new level. The first model to utilize this layout was the FXST. A new V2 motor bolted directly to the frame and a 21-inch front and 16-inch rear wheel carried chrome spokes. An ultralow saddle height of 27.5 inches teamed with a bobbed rear fender and pullback bars for a natural riding stance that was instantly comfortable.

With the debut of a new motor and chassis design for 1984, the following year was rather mild by comparison. The XL series received small changes and the XR-1000 was no longer offered. A final belt drive was installed on nearly every model in the fleet, as buyers found the system neater and quieter than the chains they replaced.

Celebrating another major biker venue, the 1992 FXDB was produced wearing graphics to highlight the 50th year of fun at Daytona Beach's Bike Week.

The final year for the fire breathing XR-1000 was 1984.

Year: 1984
Model: XR-1000
Engine: Twin-cylinder, 61 cubic inches
Transmission: Four-speed
Features: High-performance engine,
   Dell'Orto carbs, satin black
   exhaust pipes

Although first sold as a 1983 model, and still powered by the previous motor, the XR-1000 returned for a second year of sales as a 1984 model. Changes from the 1983 model included a choice of the dark silver or orange and black paint theme, and improved braking.

Despite the long list of performance features, the XR-1000's appeal was limited, with only 759 being produced for the 1984 model run. While considered by the few that bought them to be one of the sportiest Harleys ever, they would be pulled from the bench the following year.

With the passing of the XR-1000, this menacing set of blacked-out pipes would never be seen again on a factory Harley.

Alloy cylinder heads taken from the XR-750 were bolted to iron cylinders to create the XR's potent motor, and a pair of Dell'Orto carbs fed the mill.

Freshly minted for 1986 was the larger XLH-1100 Sportster. It would be sold alongside the smaller 883 version.

In 1986, the Sportsters not only got the new V2 motor in their frames, but the XL buyer had a choice of two displacements. Either 883 or 1100 were seen in the latest XLH model, providing a new level of fitment for the smaller or beginning rider. Producing 53 and 63 horsepower respectively, both versions were coupled to a four-speed gearbox.

The XLH-1100 sold for about $5,200 in 1986, which placed it more than $1,000 over its smaller XLH-883 sibling in the price line. A set of two instruments and buckhorn bars made the 1100 easier to differentiate from the smaller 883 variant.

Carrying the latest Evo motor in the frame, the revised version of the Sportster was more powerful than ever, luring new riders to the fold.

Year: 1986
Model: XLH-1100
Engine: Twin-cylinder, 1,100 cc
Transmission: Four-speed
Features: New Evo motor, dual gauges, pullback bars

The buckhorn handlebars and twin gauges made the bigger XLH easily identifiable as it sat next to its smaller sibling.

Year: 1988
Model: FXSTS
Engine: Twin-cylinder, 80 cubic inches
Transmission: Five-speed
Features: Springer front fork, wire
    wheels, birthday badges

The all-new FXSTS was introduced to celebrate the 85th birthday of Harley-Davidson.

Opposite: From the newest springer front fork to the duck-tail rear fender, the FXSTS brought a new level of "custom" to the showroom floor.

The now famous Milwaukee builder celebrated another anniversary year in 1985, and a wide range of models carried birthday trim onto the streets. Both circular and winged art could be found on the 1985 models, and all carried the digits "85" proudly.

Of the birthday badged models, the FXSTS was a brand new face in the Harley family scrapbook. The FXSTS carried a springer front fork that was reminiscent of earlier Harley machines, but had been designed using the latest in CAD technology. A set of midlevel bars reached back to the rider's hands, and a two-place pillion offered comfort for one or two people.

Harley-Davidson's 85th anniversary markings abounded, including the appliqué seen on the front fender of the FXSTS.

The FXRP was designed for use in law enforcement agencies and was utilized by many state departments.

Year: 1989
Model: FXRP
Engine: Twin-cylinder Evo, 80 cubic inches
Transmission: Five-speed
Features: Certified speedometer,
    police equipment

Introduced in 1984 models, the newest variant of Harley's V-twin motor had proven to be a tough and reliable upgrade to the previous Shovelhead.

Based on the existing FXR model, Harley-Davidson produced machines made specifically for official police department issue. The FXRP was identical in most ways to the pedestrian FXR, but was equipped with certified speedometers with "Police Special" printed on their face.

Depending on its intended use, the FXRP could be laden with a wide variety of police gear. Radios, siren, lights, and storage bins made it the perfect vehicle for patrolling the streets on a nimble machine. Many would see service as parade vehicles, while others were used on the streets, fighting crime alongside the four-door sedans.

Last seen as a 1982 model, the FXDB Sturgis returned for 1991, and now carried the Evo motor in its revised frame.

Returning to the fold for the 1991 model year was the black and red FXDB Sturgis model, now fitted with the V2 motor. The twin drive belt system was still in use. Additional changes to the FXDB's frame geometry were unique, and used only two rubber motor mounts versus the trio applied to other Harley models.

The now classic dark finish was still used to separate the Sturgis from the clan, and the Evo motor delivered new levels of power and smoothness to the born-again edition. Just over 1,500 copies of the Sturgis were produced for the 1991 model year, making it a highly prized machine today.

Year: 1991
Model FXDB Sturgis
Engine: Twin-cylinder, 80 cubic inches
Transmission: Five-speed
Features: Black and red theme,
"Sturgis" trim, dual motor mounts.

Finished in a variety of black, the motor, frame, and sheet metal of the 1991 FXDB remained as sinister as ever.

Using only two motor mounts made the 1991 FXDB truly unique in the Harley family, since most other models used a set of three to hold their Evo motors in place.

The 1993 Nostalgia, a special edition of the FLSTN, was otherwise known as the "Cow Glide."

Another landmark passed in 1993 as Harley-Davidson marked 90 years of uninterrupted production. As was expected, a series of machines graced with special birthday paint and graphics were sold, as well as a few other special models.

The FLSTN was nicknamed the "Cow Glide" for the tasteful application of furry Holstein inserts on the seat and saddlebags. The official designation was the "Nostalgia," but Cow Glide was much more entertaining.

Harley-Davidson held a huge birthday bash in Milwaukee, and over 100,000 devotees flocked to the event. It seemed that Harley's efforts to catch the Asian competition were paying off with unseen dividends.

The two-toned "fur" applied to the seat and saddlebags of the FLSTN only added to the appeal of the black and white paint scheme.

Year: 1993
Model: FLSTN "Nostalgia"
Engine: Twin-cylinder, 80 cubic inches
Transmission: Five-speed
Features: Black and white paint with
    furry "cow" inserts

Year: 1994
Model: FLHTCU
Engine: Twin-cylinder, 80 cubic inches
Transmission: Five-speed
Features: Luggage, electronics,
    long-range abilities

Taking touring to its highest level of comfort, the FLHTCU provided the rider and his passenger every amenity conceivable.

Opposite: Found at the pinnacle of Harley-Davidson's touring mounts, the FLHTCU leaves little to the imagination of the touring rider.

There are some riders for whom a quick trip around the block satisfies their needs. For others, nothing short of a multistate jaunt will do, and the FLHTCU fills their every need.

Powered by the same Evo motor found in most of the 1994 models, the FLHTCU is equipped with every comfort and convenience feature offered. Rider and passenger enjoy luxurious saddles and spacious storage cases, while electronic trickery fills every nook and cranny. The Ultra serves the demands of the long-distance rider to perfection, and sits at the top of the heap in the 1994 model lineup.

Still fed with carburetion in 1994, the Evo motor was still a potent powerplant that was delivering dependability on a daily basis.

Another new model for Harley in 1995 was the FXSTSB "Bad Boy."

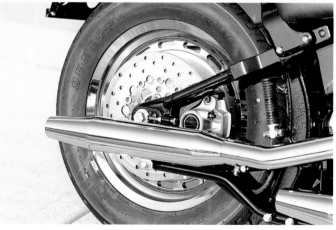

A slotted rear wheel was mostly covered by the drilled disc brake on the aft end of the Bad Boy.

The Dyna line continued to evolve, as the FXD chassis replaced the FXR. Using the revised platform, another new model was added. The FXSTSB, or "Bad Boy" was a mixture of a springer front fork, solid rear wheel, and plenty of attitude. Factory-installed forward controls, fairly low handlebars, and the evil black color scheme added up to a dramatic new look.

Combining style and function, a floating front brake rotor helped to bring the Bad Boy into the current state of affairs in the two-wheeled universe. The 80-inch Evo motor was finished in black with polished cooling fins to complement the rest of the Bad Boy's ensemble.

Factory-installed forward controls, a springer front fork, and scalloped graphics gave form and function to the FXSTSB.

Year: 1995
Model: FXSTSB Bad Boy
Engine: Twin-cylinder, 80 cubic inches
Transmission: Five-speed
Features: Springer front fork, slotted
      rear wheel, cloisonné tank badges

First sold as a 1990 model, the FLSTF remained in the lineup in 1997, although it now carried more typical paint schemes.

A modernized winged logo graced the sides of the Fat Boy's wide fuel tank.

First sold as a 1990 model, the FLSTF, or "Fat Boy" continued its run of popularity in 1997. The wide "beach bars" were still used, as were the solid wheels at both ends of the low-slung FL.

Cosmetic changes were the only revisions to the 1997 editions. But with a runaway success, why mess with the formula? The original all-silver motif had been replaced in 1991, and every year saw different hues being applied to the sheet metal of the Fat Boy. The winged tank trim remained the same.

Year: 1997
Model: FLSTF Fat Boy
Engine: Twin-cylinder, 80 cubic inches
Transmission: Five-speed
Features: Solid wheels, wide bars

Helping to celebrate 95 years of production, the FLSTS was sold in the official birthday hues in 1998.

Year: 1998
Model: 95th Anniversary
    Editions
Engine: Twin-cylinder,
    80 cubic inches
Transmission: Five-speed
Features: 95th Anniversary
    colors and badges

Considered the King of the line, the FLHTCUI possessed all the features required for riding across town or across the country.

Another birthday year was celebrated in 1998 as Harley-Davidson marked 95 years of trusted service. In typical fashion, a series of specially trimmed models were sold alongside the other available hues and trim levels. A returning model was found in the FLTR Road Glide, which carried a frame-mounted fairing along with a wide complement of accessories that befitted the touring bike. Variations on the Road King theme grew as a Classic edition joined the existing version. Detailed tooling on the leather helped to distinguish the Classic from the standard Road King. It could also be fitted with fuel injection or a carburetor.

After some dark days in the 1970s, Harley found itself in an enviable position as a market leader. Sales of the big twin machines had swelled to unforeseen proportions as new models were created with every passing year. With a successful track record under its belt, the Motor Company hoped to continue expanding, and planned for another motor revision in 1999.

Another entrant in the birthday parade was the FXDWG, also trimmed in anniversary colors.

Chapter 7: New Times, New Motor

The introduction of the Evo motor in the 1984 models ushered Harley-Davidson into a period of prosperity that was more than likely a surprise to even the Motor Company itself. Rapidly expanding production numbers struggled to keep pace with buyers as the builder rolled through its 90th and 95th anniversary years. There seemed to be no end to the demand for the legendary V-twin powered machines, and with this surge of buyers came a cry for more power. The V2 edition had taken a great leap and delivered on the promise of greater dependability along with added horsepower, but this trend only added fuel to the fire, with riders clamoring for even more of both commodities. Instead of merely tweaking the Evo mill, Harley again turned its attention to the R&D department and created another breed of their classic 45-degree motor.

The computer age played a huge role in the development of the latest mill, each design involving thousands of hours spent in the virtual world. Pre-testing of every major component was done on powerful computers long before they were created in alloy to become real.

The Twin-Cam 88 engine, which shared only 18 bits from the previous variant, saw its first use in 1999. Getting a bump from 1,340 to 1,450 cc, the newest motor was the biggest Harley-Davidson had ever offered. Revised internal cooling and beefier external fins on the cylinders do their part to keep the higher-displacement mill under control. Higher compression now would require premium fuel, but the added power was worth the cost at the pumps. Spinning the bigger pistons was a crankshaft that weighed in at 2 pounds more than the one it replaced, but durability was still a requirement of the fresh design. Lurking behind the football-shaped air cleaner was either a Keihin carburetor or sequential fuel injection, depending on which model was purchased. The fruits of their labors were proven when horsepower ratings claimed 10 additional ponies. The new "Fathead" motor was warmly received by the media and public alike and would serve the market well for years to come.

While 1999 was the first year for the new Twin-Cam 88 motor, not every machine would receive the latest powerplant. The smaller Sportster clan still featured the Evo mill but a revised Custom model was offered. The Softail models were also still powered by the Evo motor, and an FXST Standard was now sold along with the FXSTB Night Train. The Night Train was another blacked-out version, while the Standard was pitched as an entry level model. The entire Dyna and FL catalog featured the latest TC 88 mill, but only a few were fed by fuel injection for the latest year.

Harley's Twin-Cam 88 appeared in 1999, but in an effort to continue their winning ways on the sales floor, an improved version would appear in the 2007 catalog. In a fast changing world of two-wheeled toys, the Motor Company was learning that resting on their laurels only lost them customers and market share.

The larger displacement motor was also connected to a six-speed transmission named the Cruise Drive. The bigger motor and added gear took away a few of the niggling complaints that were being heard by potential buyers of the iconic brand. Now they were fully vested into the modern specifications of the latest hardware, all the while retaining their foothold in the classic, V-twin design that made them THE Motor Company.

The FLHRI Road King was one of the 1999 models that benefited from the use of the all-new Twin-Cam 88 motor with fuel injection as an option.

The FXSTB was a new model for 1999 that carried the Bad Boy's dark theme a step further.

Year: 1999
Model: FXSTB Night Train
Engine: Twin-cylinder, 80 cubic inches
Transmission: Five-speed
Features: Blacked-out motor

Adding to the mix of models for the 1999 model year was the all-black FXSTB, otherwise known as the Night Train. By combining visual clues that were cloaked in black, along with a smattering of glittering chrome, the Night Train took over where the Bad Boy left off.

Although a new model, the Night Train was still fitted with the previous version of the V2 motor, and not the new Twin-Cam 88. The 80-inch motor was finished in a variety of black paints, some smooth and others textured. A two-into-two exhaust was all chrome to offset the otherwise darkened hues.

Carrying the dark motif to its furthest extreme, the Night Train was finished in a variety of black paints, along with a few hints of chrome.

Not every model in the 1999 lineup got the new TC-88 mill, and the Night Train was one that retained the V2 motor from the previous year.

The new millennium introduced catalog-wide improvements in braking, batteries, and bearings, with revisions to existing models and another new name added to the list.

The Softail models were assembled using a more rigid frame design, and the new Deuce also had the latest chassis. The 34-percent bump in stiffness provided better handling in the Deuce, along with an elongated fuel tank and a straight-line rear fender. A spoke front wheel was joined by a solid rear hoop, while a chrome version of the fathead motor delivered the power.

The solid rear wheel was contrasted by the lace unit used up front, and the straight lines of the rear fender delivered a new style to the Deuce.

The Deuce held the latest Twin-Cam 88 motor in its flanks along with a style that was all its own.

Opposite: Fresh off the drawing board for the 2000 model year was the Deuce. The FXSTD had distinctive sheet metal, exhaust pipes, and a solid wheel beneath the bobbed rear fender.

Year: 2000
Model: FXSTD Deuce
Engine: Twin-cylinder, 88 cubic inch, Twin-Cam
Transmission: Five-speed
Features: Bobbed rear fender, solid rear wheel

The FLTR remained in the lineup for 2001 and was still equipped with frame-mounted fairing and hard-sided saddlebags.

Year: 2001
Model: FLTR
Engine: Twin-cylinder, 88 cubic inches, Twin-Cam
Transmission: Five-speed
Features: Available in regular or Screamin'
　　　　Eagle versions.

For the rider who wanted a bit more punch from his touring mount, Harley offered up the Screamin' Eagle FLTR in 2001.

The entire line for 2001 was revised, although most changes were minor. Of the big FL models, the FLTR still provided the buyer with a great all-around machine that was equally proficient at home or on the open road. The frame-mounted half fairing provided substantial protection from the elements and held an improved audio system behind the low windscreen.

For the FLTR rider who demanded even more power, it was offered in a Screamin' Eagle version that delivered higher horsepower from a bigger motor and carried flashier graphics on the body work.

Introduced as a 1999 model, the FXSTB Night Train was an instant success among buyers of the FX models.

While 1999 saw the introduction of the Night Train, at that time, the older V2 motor was still used in the FXSTB. The 2002 edition of the bike found the newest Twin-Cam 88 bolted into the frame rails.

The same black motif was applied to the 2002 version, while the TC-88 motor brought more power and smoothness to the creation. The Night Train's low saddle height and low drag bars placed the rider in an aggressive stance, but the posture fit the black machine's personality well.

Year: 2002
Model: FXSTB Night Train
Engine: Twin-cylinder, 88 cubic inches, Twin-Cam
Transmission: Five-speed
Features: New TC-88 motor installed for 2002

Not only was the FXSTB cloaked in a veil of black, but it carried the latest Twin-Cam 88 motor in the frame rails.

With hopes of capturing a bigger slice of the market, Harley made a bold step in introducing the VRSCA, or V-Rod, for 2002.

Year: 2002
Model: VRSCA V-Rod
Engine: Twin-cylinder, 60-degree,
    liquid-cooled
Transmission: Five-speed
Features: Fuel injection, 115
    horsepower motor

Styling on the V-Rod was also quite radical for Harley and included this tri-faced instrument pod that rested at the end of a tapered neck.

Going with a liquid-cooled, 60-degree V-twin motor was a gamble, but a new level of high-tech trickery was achieved by doing so.

The year 2002 would see the introduction of a radical new motorcycle from Harley-Davidson. With a desire to capture some market share that they had been missing, Harley chose a high-tech path when creating the VRSCA V-Rod.

Not only would the new mount be powered by a liquid-cooled motor, it would deviate from the standard 45-degree layout with an angle of 60 degrees between the cylinders. A similar mill had been installed on the racing-only VR-1000 in 1994, but neither the cycle nor the motor gained universal acceptance. The 69-inch V-Rod motor produced 115 horsepower right off the showroom floor, and set a new standard for the Motor Company. Four valve heads and dual overhead cams provided the necessary breathing, while sequential, multiport fuel injection sent the required fuel and air mix where it was needed.

Rolling on a 67.5-inch wheelbase was another first for Harley, and the frame was of the perimeter configuration, supplanting the more typical steel backbone layout. Space age techniques were employed to form the sections of the frame, and the result of these efforts was a frame that was more rigid than ever seen before on a Harley. Solid wheels at both ends complemented the gleaming alloy finish of the sheet metal on the 2002 models. A pair of graceful, yet massive exhaust pipes combined form with function at a new level of art. Fuel was stored in a tank that was mounted beneath the saddle, keeping the center of gravity low and allowing a sleek faux tank to live in the expected location.

Another new model in the 2002
catalog was the FXDWG3. A blend
of style and unique features set this
factory custom apart from the crowd.

Year: **2002**
Model **FXDWG3**
Engine: **Twin-cylinder, 88 cubic inches, Twin-Cam**
Transmission: **Five-speed**
Features: **Sport fairings, "ostrich" saddle**

The use of a small bikini fairing on the FXDWG3 led the way and was matched with a small chin spoiler mounted low on the frame rails.

While being the most radical, the V-Rod was not the only change in the 2002 catalog. A fresh attempt at building a factory custom appeared in the shape of the FXDWG3. Building on the success of the Dyna Wide Glide platform, the designers added a set of upper and lower bikini fairings, flashy graphics, and simulated ostrich upholstery on the two-place saddle.

Cast wheels were found under both tires, and a pair of large disc brakes hauled the FXDWG3 down from speed.

The big twin range was not the only to gain fresh talent, and the 2002 XL-883R carried the Sportster colors proudly.

Year: 2002
Model: XL-883R
Engine: Twin-cylinder, 883 cc
Transmission: Five-speed
Features: Racing colors, performance engine

There remained a certain faction of riders who desired a slightly smaller Harley, but weren't ready to sacrifice performance. For this crowd, the 2002 XL-883R model filled their needs.

Enhanced speed was derived by using a variety of subtle modifications inside the motor along with a specially tuned two-into-one exhaust. The finish on the hot rod motor was both black and polished for a tasteful blend.

The orange and black paint and graphics were direct descendents of the mighty XR-750, which had prowled and dominated the tracks nearly 30 years earlier.

The color scheme smacked of the previous XR-750, and the blacked-out motor was tuned for maximum performance.

With a debut in 2000, the Deuce remained in the lineup to ring in the 100th year of production for Harley.

Year: 2003
Model: FXSTD Deuce
Engine: Twin-cylinder, 88 cubic inches,
    Twin-Cam
Transmission: Five-speed
Features: 100th anniversary colors

In keeping with tradition, the 2003 models would trumpet the anniversary of the Motor Company in a big way, with special trim, color, and badges to mark the 100th year of production from the now fabled Milwaukee builder. Along with the specially trimmed editions, mechanical alterations were seen, but were kept to a minimum as the entire city celebrated the benchmark birthday.

With three years of production under its belt, the Deuce could now be fitted with a variety of factory accessories, as witnessed by the windscreen applied to this example.

A set of staggered mufflers capped off the exhaust of the Deuce, and was just one of its distinctive features.

The Twin-Cam 88 motor continued to improve, and delivered a new level of power and smoothness.

The Fat Boy was back for another year, and the silver sheet metal of this 2004 looks similar to the original 1990 edition.

Year: 2004
Model: FLSTF Fat Boy
Engine: Twin-cylinder, 88 cubic inches, Twin-Cam
Transmission: Five-speed
Features: Solid wheels, wide handlebars

One of the most popular models ever created by Harley-Davidson, the FLSTF, or Fat Boy, was back for another round in 2004. Only subtle alterations had been made to its appearance for the latest model year, including an all-silver sheet metal array teamed with a black frame.

The newest editions of the Fat Boy did, however, benefit from the installation of the Twin-Cam 88 motor. The added displacement was a welcome addition, and both civilians and the media were impressed by the motor's smoothness.

A wide set of handlebars had become a hallmark of the Fat Boy and played heavily into the attitude of the model.

The V-Rod was now offered in a variety of hues, replacing the original gleaming silver finish.

The years following the birthday blowout were fairly quiet, as the line was treated to more incremental improvements. The 2004 V-Rod was offered in different hues, including some two-tone combinations, and a mostly black model was dubbed the VRSCB.

With its debut as a 2002 model, the V-Rod encapsulated a raft of modern technologies into a radical new machine for the traditional Milwaukee maker. The potent 60-degree, liquid-cooled motor was still in place with only cosmetic enhancements on the 2004 models.

Cloaked in a more menacing set of colors, the 2004 VRSCB forced the V-Rod buyer to make another choice before riding one home.

Two shades of silver set apart by barbed wire trim really gave the VRSCB a purposeful look.

Year: 2004
Model: VRSCA/VRSCB V-Rod
Engine: Twin-cylinder, 60-degree,
    liquid-cooled
Transmission: Five-speed
Features: VRSCB model carries altered
    graphics and fresh hues

The year 2005 saw another entry made in the Softail lineup as the Deluxe name rolled onto the sales floors.

Year: 2005
Model: FLSTN Deluxe
Engine: Twin-cylinder, 88 cubic inches, Twin-Cam
Transmission: Five-speed
Features: Full coverage fenders, whitewall tires, driving lights

Two more versions of the Softail would appear in 2005, making the choice even more difficult for the Harley buyer. The FLSTN Deluxe carried the newest Twin-Cam 88B motor in its frame and was dressed in full fenders and wide whitewall tires. Dazzling chrome spokes were fitted into the latest Profile rims, which mounted to the tire without the usual lip around the perimeter.

A classic winged tank badge makes the Deluxe easy to spot, as does the "Deluxe" script on the front fender.

One of the many unique features of the FLSTN were the winged badges applied to each side of the fuel tank.

Leading the way on the Deluxe were the classic driving lights that flanked the large headlight.

The Springer Classic was another new face in the 2005 catalogs, and captured the spirit of several past models.

Year: 2005
Model: FLSTC Springer Classic
Engine: Twin-cylinder, 88 cubic inches,
   Twin-Cam
Transmission: Five-speed
Features: Springer front forks,
   retro front fender

A dominant feature on any springer model is the chrome suspension components mounted to the upper portion of the forks.

The second new entry into the Softail clan was the FLSTC Springer Classic. At the leading edge of the design were a springer front fork in the steering head and a wide set of beach bars. Drop your seat onto the superlow 25.9-inch saddle and place your boots on the spacious floorboards for a classic and comfortable ride.

The matching saddlebags are joined by a vintage style front fender decorated with chrome tear drops. The buyer could also choose from a variety of solid or two-tone color combinations.

2006 Super Glide

Marking the return of the 1971 FX model, Harley brought us the Super Glide for 2006.

Year: 2006
Model: Super Glide
Engine: Twin-cylinder, 88 cubic inches, Twin-Cam
Transmission: Six-Speed "Cruise Drive"
Features: 35th anniversary badges; white, red, and blue paint; new six-speed gearbox

Visual references like the number 1 on the fuel tank were strong reminders of the bike that appeared 35 years past.

Harley-Davidson had introduced their unusually styled FX in 1971, and to mark the 35th birthday of the model, reinvented the wheel with the release of the 2006 Super Glide. Decked out in a similar white scheme with red and blue trim, the new Super Glide carried a traditional rear fender in place of the controversial boat tail used on the 1971. Cosmetic details like the red, white, and blue number 1 on the fuel tank were joined by 35th anniversary badges on the chrome oil tank. For the first time, a six-speed gearbox has been added to the Super Glide with Harley's new "Cruise Drive."

As a tribute to the 1971 FX, the white paint was trimmed with panels of red and blue on the 2006 Super Glide.

The chrome oil tank was adorned with a 35th anniversary badge, helping to make this 2006 edition truly special.

INDEX